ABSTRACT

The Sexual Assault Among Latinas (SALAS) Study adds to the literature by using a national sample of Latino women to determine the extent of sexual victimization alone and the overlap of sexual victimization with other forms of victimization. Additional distinguishing components of SALAS includes an investigation of formal and informal help-seeking responses; inclusion of culturally - relevant variables such as religiosity, gender role ideology and acculturation in relation to victimization and help-seeking; and assessing the psychosocial impact of sexual victimization on psychological distress and posttraumatic symptomatology.

A national sample of 2,000 adult Latino women living in high-density Latino neighborhoods participated. Trained professionals from an experienced survey research firm conducted interviews over the phone in either English or Spanish, from May through September 2008. Respondents were queried about lifetime victimization, help-seeking efforts, acculturation, religiosity, gender role ideology, trauma symptoms, and post-traumatic symptoms. Respondents were on average 47.76 years of age and largely foreign-born (72.4%).

The lifetime rate of sexual victimization was 17.2% with 87.5% of sexual victims experiencing another form of victimization (physical, threat, stalking or witness) within their lifetime. Sexual victimization mostly commonly occurred with physical victimization in childhood (47.3%) and threatened victimization in adulthood (55.9%). Victims of child sexual assault were more likely to experience any form of adult victimization (OR = 4.59, $p < .001$) than non-victims. The rate of formal help-seeking was 21% and the rate of informal help-seeking was 60% among those who selected a sexual victimization as their most distressing event. Medical attention was mostly commonly sought among injured sexual victims (41%) and friends (31.7%) and family members (30.9%) were the most common confidants. Anglo acculturation was associated with increased odds of sexual victimization (OR = .98, p < .001) and formal help-seeking (OR = 1.10, p = .04). PTSD and trauma symptoms were associated with total number of sexual assaults, but best explained by total victimization count.

Latino women face substantial sexual victimization and other forms of victimization at each life stage. However, linkages to services are still weak and can be addressed by building on the strengths and cultural traditions of Latino women. We recommend using medical settings as an intervention point and educating the larger community of available services, so that family members and friends can educate each other. The significant overlap in victimization found calls for thorough assessments in clinical settings and more refined measurement in future research.

TABLE OF CONTENTS

EXECUTIVE SUMMARY

Synopsis of the Problem

As of 2004, Latinos constituted the largest and most rapidly growing minority group in the United States (Pew Research Center, 2005). The large numbers and growth of this segment of the population merits research attention to evaluate how these individuals are affected by interpersonal violence. Specifically, we aimed to investigate the role of sexual violence among Latino women, the impact of victimization, and what services and resources they pursue.

Sexual violence research has evaluated the incidence and prevalence of the problem, the psychosocial impact of sexual violence, associated public health and medical consequences, and how it plays a role in revictimization risk for subsequent sexual victimization (Banyard, Williams, & Siegel, 2001; Briere & Elliott, 2003; Browne & Finkelhor, 1986; Classen, Palesh, & Aggarwal, 2005; Elliott, Mok, & Briere, 2004; Golding, 1994; Golding, Stein, Siegel, Burman, & Sorenson, 1988). However, this research has largely ignored the Latino population and left a void in our knowledge of how sexual violence impact Latino women. As an example, in searching the published literature on PsycINFO that looks at interpersonal victimization, approximately only 1% focuses on Latinos.

When examining the research that does focus on Latino women, significant gaps need to be filled. Much of the literature that examines interpersonal violence among Latino women typically focuses on partner violence or sexual violence. However, this line of research has overlooked other forms of victimization that may be experienced along with partner violence or sexual violence. This limitation potentially overestimates the impact of any specific form of violence by not accounting for other forms of co-occurring victimization, (e.g., stalking, threats, etc.), which we term polyvictimization (Finkelhor, Ormrod, & Turner, 2007a). In addition, without evaluating other forms of victimization, we are unable to see the full spectrum of violence that Latino women may experience.

Another key aspect of victimization research among Latino women is the need to evaluate help-seeking efforts and address cultural issues that may play a salient role in victimization, and both formal and informal help seeking behaviors. The research on sexual violence suggests that it is an underreported issue (Finkelhor, Hotaling, Lewis, & Smith, 1990; Finkelhor & Ormrod, 2001; Widom & Morris, 1997). Therefore, it is important to evaluate what formal services victims of sexual violence attempt to seek out and what role cultural factors such as acculturation, religiosity, immigration status, and gender roles might play in their willingness to seek services. Formal help-seeking includes reporting victimization to police, obtaining restraining orders, seeking legal remedies, getting medical services, and seeking counseling or social services. Informal help seeking, which literature suggests occurs more frequently than formal help-seeking (Ingram, 2007; Lewis, West, Bautista, Greenberg, & Done-Perez, 2005), typically includes behaviors such as talking to friends and family or seeking counsel from the clergy. Understanding these help-seeking behaviors is crucial as these types of support and actions often help taper or overcome the negative sequelae of sexual violence.

In line with previous research on sexual violence, research focusing on Latino women needs to evaluate the psychosocial impact of victimization. This should focus on symptomatology that has been associated with victimization including posttraumatic reactions, depression, anxiety, anger/irritability, and dissociation (Anderson, Yasenik, & Ross, 1993; Briere & Elliott, 2003; Browne & Finkelhor, 1986; Neumann, Houskamp, Pollock, & Briere, 1996; Nishith, Mechanic, & Resick, 2000). Specifically, it is important to evaluate the role of sexual violence on psychological distress as well as the role that polyvictimization may have and the impact that cultural issues may have on victimization and post-victimization reactions.

Given the above-stated research limitations and areas that need further exploration, we designed the Sexual Assault Among Latinas (SALAS) study. This study aimed to examine interpersonal victimization among a national sample of Latino women, particularly focusing on help-seeking behaviors, culturally relevant factors, and psychosocial impacts.

Purpose

SALAS aimed to fulfill the following goals:

Goal 1: Determine extent of sexual victimization in a sample of adult Latino females.

Goal 2: Determine the coexistence of other forms of victimization among those sexually victimized and the risk for subsequent victimization.

Goal 3: Examine formal service utilization among sexually victimized Latino women.

Goal 4: Examine informal help-seeking among sexually victimized Latino women.

Goal 5: Examine culturally-relevant factors associated with experience and responses to sexual violence.

Goal 6: Determine the psychosocial impact of sexual victimization on Latino women.

Research Design

Participants

The SALAS study, with data collected between May and September 2008, assessed the victimization experiences of a national sample of 2,000 Latino women living in the United States. Trained professionals from an experienced survey research firm conducted the interviews over the phone in either English or Spanish.

The study entrance criteria were that participants needed to be women over the age of 18 who self-identified as Latino (either foreign or U.S. born), and whose primary language was either English or Spanish. The total sample consisted of 2,000 participants with the majority of participants (90%) living in high-density Latino areas (80% or higher) based on U.S. Census data. The minimum response rate for the sample was 30.7%. The average age of the participants was 47.76 years of age. Approximately 63% of the sample has a high school education or less. The majority of participants (61%) were U.S. citizens (either U.S. born or naturalized) and 71.5% of the sample conducted the interview in Spanish (see Table 1). The participants in the sample were predominantly immigrants from Mexico or of Mexican descent (67.1% and 89.5% respectively), with the second most common immigrant group being from Cuba (18%). Detailed ethnicity data are presented in Table 2.

In comparing our sample to available U.S. Census figures on Latinos, we have a notably higher median age, which was likely inflated by our screening procedures that did not allow for participants under the age of 18. Our sample has a higher rate of a high school education and beyond, a similar proportion of being married, and a smaller proportion of being born in the U.S. or being U.S. citizens (Guzman, 2001; Ramirez, 2004; U.S. Census Bureau, 2000). In evaluating ethnic background, the SALAS sample has a larger proportion of individuals of Mexican and Cuban descent (U.S. Census Bureau, 2000).

Measures

The SRBI methods report in the appendix provides a complete version of the survey. The participants were asked a number of demographic questions including age, country of origin, whether they immigrated to the United States, their preferred language, sexual orientation, education level, employment status, household income, housing status, and relationship status

8

(e.g., married, single, etc.). In addition, regional information was obtained from census tract information linked to the random digit dial (RDD) blocks.

We evaluated lifetime victimization using and adapted version of the Lifetime Trauma and Victimization History (LTVH) questionnaire (Widom, Dutton, Czaja, & DuMont, 2005) which asks about a broad range of potentially traumatic experiences. We limited the questions to those focusing on interpersonal victimization including stalking, physical assaults, weapon assaults, physical assaults in childhood, threats, threats with weapons, sexual assault, attempted sexual assault, sexual fondling, kidnapping, and witnessed victimization.

The Help Seeking Questionnaire (HSQ) was developed specifically for this study which was adapted from surveys used in two other large-scale studies (Block, 2000; Gelles & Straus, 1988). This questionnaire asked about the actions taken by respondents after identifying the most distressing incident of victimization. The questions asked about both formal (e.g., reporting to police, getting medical care, seeking legal remedies) and informal (e.g., talking to friends, family, or the clergy) forms of help-seeking.

The three main cultural variables evaluated were religiosity/spirituality, acculturation, and sex role characteristics. Religiosity was evaluated using the Brief Multidimensional Measure of Religiousness/Spirituality (BMMRS), which was designed to study religiousness and spirituality in health-related studies (Pargament, Koenig, & Perez, 2000). Participant acculturation was evaluated using the Brief Acculturation Rating Scale of Mexican-Americans – II (Brief ARSMA – II). The Brief ARSMA -II assesses both minority and majority cultural identity (Bauman, 2005). Sex-typed personality characteristics were measured using the Short Bem Sex Role Inventory (BSRI- Short Form) by asking participants to report the degree to which 30 adjectives - 10 masculine, 10 feminine and 10 neutral items (Bem, 1981). Two instruments were used to evaluate trauma-related symptomatology, the Trauma Symptom Inventory (TSI) and the Posttraumatic Stress Disorder Checklist (PCL). The TSI is a 100-item instrument that evaluates posttraumatic and trauma related symptomatology in adults (Briere, 1995). For this study we used the Anxious Arousal, Depression, Anger/Irritability, and Dissociation scales of the TSI. The PCL is an instrument that evaluates the severity of Posttraumatic Stress Disorder (PTSD) symptomatology (Weathers, Litz, Herman, Huska, & Keane, 1993), covering the three main symptom clusters of the DSM-IV criteria for PTSD: reexperiencing, numbing/avoidance, and hyperarousal (American Psychiatric Association, 2000).

Procedures

Probability samples of households with telephones were generated using a random digit dial method (RDD). This methodology seeks to draw a random sample numbers using Census-based hundred-blocks. For SALAS, the sample was from telephone numbers stratified by Hispanic household density per hundred block. Eligible residential households within the total sample were then selected.

When a residential household was reached, the interviewer asked about the total number of age-eligible Latino women in the household. When an eligible individual was identified and agreed to participate they were asked the various study instruments in their preferred language (either English or Spanish). Upon completing the survey, participants were asked if they felt distressed and were offered a support hotline or callback to follow up with them. The study's principal investigator, who is a bilingual licensed clinical psychologist, called the follow-up cases if necessary. On follow-up calls, it was ensured that the individual was no longer distressed and they were provided with additional support information if needed (e.g., local social service agencies, etc.). Approximately 1% of the sample required follow-up. Upon completion of the survey, participants were paid $10 for their participation.

An experienced survey research firm with specialization in doing surveys that ask about sensitive subjects (e.g., interpersonal violence) conducted the interviews using a Computer Assisted Telephone Interview (CATI) system. The interviewers, all female, were specifically trained on the SALAS survey and closely supervised during the data collection process. The Institutional Review Board (IRB) of Northeastern University authorized all study procedures with subsequent analyses also being approved by the IRB of The Pennsylvania State University.

Key Findings

Sexual Victimization Rates and Co-Morbid Victimization

- The rate of sexual victimization for the sample was 17.2% (22.2% weighted).

- 8.8% of the sample experienced a completed sexual assault, 8.9% experienced attempted sexual assault, and 11.4% experienced fondling or forced touch.

- 7.6% of the sample experienced at least one adulthood sexual assault and 12.2% of the sample experienced at least one childhood sexual assault.

- Perpetration of sexual violence against women in adulthood was primarily by individuals known to the victim with a partner or spouse (44.1% of adult sexual victimization) or someone else known to the victim (48.7% of adult sexual victimization) being the most common perpetrator.

- For victimization experienced in childhood, other relatives and non-family individuals known to the victim are the most common perpetrators (42.6% and 38.1% respectively).

- Of the women who experienced sexual assault, 87.5% of them experienced at least one other type of victimization with physical violence being the most common form of co-occurring victimization (60.2%) and witnessed violence being the least common form of co-occurring victimization (45.1%).

- The most common co-occurring form of victimization in childhood was physical violence (47.3%) with threats being the last common co-occurring form of victimization (22.4%).

- Co-occurring forms of victimization for Latino women who experienced sexual violence in adulthood, ranged from 55.9% (threat) to 23.7% (witness).

- The highest revictimization risk for victims of sexual assault was experiencing threat in adulthood with victims of sexual abuse having more than four and a half times the odds of experiencing threat in adulthood.

- Victims of child sexual abuse (CSA) had 4.3 times the odds of experiencing sexual violence in adulthood.

- Latino women's physical victimization rate was 22.2%, stalking rate was 18.2%, threat rate was 21.1%, and witnessed violence was 20.1%.

Help-seeking

- Of the women who experienced sexual victimization, two-thirds of them (66.5%) selected this as the incident to focus on for help-seeking; that is, reported it as most distressing.

- Approximately 21% of the respondents sought one or more types of formal help.

- The most common type of formal help-seeking (41%) was medical services among women who reported injuries.

- Criminal justice responses were not commonly sought with only 6.6% of women contacting police, 7.1% obtaining a restraining order, and 6.1% pressing criminal charges.

- About 10% of women sought help from a social service agency.

- When rating the helpfulness of formal services, victims tended to be more satisfied with the court process than with police services (average rating 3.0 versus 2.4 on a scale from 1 to 4). Medical centers and mental health, abuse/trauma, and domestic violence counseling were all highly rated (average score 4.5). However, these results are cautiously interpreted as they are based on a very small number of respondents.

- For women who reported to police, almost a quarter of the women reported that charging or arresting the person would be the way to improve police service. For the courts, taking the report more seriously was the most commonly reported way that courts could improve. Finally, for medical services, providing counseling/offering advice and reporting the abuse were two ways that were most frequently cited as how to improve.

- When asked about reasons for not seeking help, fear of offender and being too young were the top two reasons for not getting help from police or the courts. In contrast, shame and other reasons were the most common reason for not getting medical help while not thinking of getting help and not knowing of any were the most frequently cited reasons for not getting help from social service agencies.

- Formal help-seeking was unrelated to any of the measured psychological symptoms.

- In total, 58.3% of women who experienced sexual assault sought informal help.

- Disclosure of sexual abuse was most often to friends (31.7%) and parents (30.9%).

- When asked as to how helpfulness of informal sources could have been improved, being more supportive was the most commonly cited reason (42.3%).

- The reason most often cited for not getting informal help was shame (31.8%), with "didn't think of it" being the next most commonly cited (19.3%) reason.

- When examining the relationship between help-seeking and psychological variables, total victimization was associated with an increase in posttraumatic symptoms and depression, while informal help-seeking was associated with a decrease in depression.

Cultural Factors Associated with Victimization and Help-seeking

- Being an immigrant is associated with decreased odds of sexual victimization so that Latino women who are immigrants to the United States are less likely to report being sexually assaulted.

- Anglo acculturation is associated with increased odds of sexual victimization, suggesting that women who are more acculturated to the United States culture are at greater risk of sexual victimization.

- Older women were less likely to report sexual violence and women of higher socioeconomic status were more likely to experience sexual assault.

- Masculine sex role, positive religious coping, and negative religious coping were the cultural factors significantly associated with mental health variables for sexually victimized Latino women. Specifically masculine sex role was associated with increased levels of PTSD symptomatology, anger, and anxiety. Positive religious coping was associated with a decrease in depression while negative religious coping was associated with an increase in PTSD symptomatology, depression, and anxiety.

- When focusing on the role of cultural factors and help-seeking for sexually victimized Latino women, only Anglo acculturation was associated with a significantly increased likelihood of seeking out social services.

- There was little impact from cultural factors on informal help-seeking with none of the cultural factors being associated with the likelihood of getting informal help across any of the different categories of individuals.

Psychological Impact of Sexual Victimization

- Sexual violence in childhood, in adulthood, the total number of sexual victimization experiences, and the total different number of victimization events were all associated with the different forms of psychological distress, including PTSD symptomatology, depression, anxiety, anger, and dissociation, at the bivariate level.

- The total number of sexual victimization experiences was consistently a significant predictor of increased symptomatology across all the measured forms of psychological distress.

- Experiences of childhood sexual abuse were significantly associated with increased level of anger and dissociation while adult sexual victimization was also associated with increased levels of anger and dissociation in addition to also contributing to increased levels of depression.

- In regression analyses that examine the role of total number of sexual victimization experiences while taking into account that total number of overall victimization experiences (including other forms of violence such as physical assaults, threats, and stalking) sexual victimization is no longer a significant predictor, with only total overall victimization significantly predicting each of the different forms of psychological distress.

Conclusions

The study points to a number of overlooked factors when evaluating sexual violence against Latino women. First, a significant proportion of these women experienced lifetime sexual victimization. Interestingly, an overwhelming number of sexually victimized women experienced more than one type of sexual victimization or other forms of interpersonal violence, suggesting that focusing only on a particular sexual assault event may overlook the complete victimization profile. Furthermore, as previous research has found, sexual victimization in childhood was a risk factor for revictimization in adulthood. However, mostly absent from prior research is that sexual violence was a risk factor for revictimization across multiple forms of interpersonal violence, including stalking, physical assault, threats, and witnessed violence.

Consistent with other studies, sexually victimized women infrequently engaged in formal help-seeking efforts such as calling police, getting social services, or using legal remedies. Our findings point to a number of reasons that could contribute to this including lack of material/economic resources and linguistic isolation (the sample predominantly preferred Spanish for communication). Results also point to a practical approach to help seeking in that increased victimization led to an increased likelihood of seeking services while immediate physical harm led to a greater likelihood of seeking medical services.

While informal help-seeking was a more likely to occur than formal help-seeking, there was still approximately one third of women who did not report their victimization to anyone. Friends and family were the most frequently reported resource for informal help. However, these results point to a significant lack of disclosure around sexual violence. This is consistent with prior research on disclosure, suggesting that Latino women, like women from other cultural

16

groups, are hesitant to come forward around victimization, and are particularly unlikely to seek out formal services or legal options.

Cultural analysis provides interesting results regarding how variables unique to Latino women may play a role in victimization. Specifically, immigrant women were less likely to report sexual violence while more Anglo acculturated women were more likely to report sexual victimization. Consistent with other research, this suggests that traditional Latino culture may be protective of victimization. Some of the traditional gender roles and familial norms may decrease the risk of violence, while, inversely, changing cultural values and roles may create acculturative stress resulting in increased risk for victimization. The friction between traditional Latino and Anglo values may promote tension in the family and lead to violence. These explanations need to be taken in the context of possible methodological factors; specifically that U.S. born and more acculturated women are more willing to disclose victimization on a phone survey.

Help-seeking was also impacted by cultural factors, specifically Anglo acculturation. Women with greater levels of acculturation were more likely to seek out formal help. This has two potential explanations. From the standpoint of cultural fit, it is more socially acceptable to tell someone unknown about victimization in mainstream American culture. From a resources perspective, more acculturated women may have greater knowledge about, and feel more comfortable obtaining, available services.

While sexual victimization was significantly associated with various psychological distress variables, supporting a large body of literature, the impact of different forms of victimization overwhelmed this effect. When the total number of different forms of victimization is taken into account, sexual victimization ceases to uniquely predict psychological distress. The overall victimization of women drives psychological sequelae, not sexual violence by itself. Focusing solely on sexual victimization without taking into account other victimization experiences may overestimate the impact of sexual violence on psychological distress and miss an opportunity to appropriately provide services to victims of sexual violence.

There are a number of key policy implications from this study. Service providers need to be aware of sexual violence dynamics among Latino women including predominant perpetration by known or familial assailants, high rates of polyvictimization and revictimization, and the likelihood that services will be sought out following an acutely traumatic event or after increased/chronic victimization. This suggests that compartmentalizing services may be detrimental to victims in that having separate domestic violence and sexual abuse hotlines potentially discourages them from getting help. Promoting services that are generally focused on interpersonal violence rather than on a particular type of victimization may improve the willingness of victims to come forward.

Formal service outlets have a number of areas where they can promote victim's willingness and ability to report victimization. These would include having Spanish-speaking victim advocates to help educate and navigate the legal system, increased protections for victims from perpetrators, and increased outreach and education efforts into the Latino community. A key entry point may be medical services, perhaps following a Sexual Assault Nurse Examiner (SANE) model. Following this model, a sexual assault specialist can work with women when they come in for medical help to provide rape crisis center information, victim advocates, and connection to law enforcement. As is the case with other services, bilingual resources are a key component.

The results from this study also indicate an increased need for public awareness and education. Many victims were simply unaware of the availability of services; existing service agencies may serve as educators and providers of public information within the Latino community. These efforts might be more effective if they are not only aimed at victims, but their families and friends, educating them on how to respond to a disclosure of abuse. Friends and family, the most commonly sought informal resource, can serve as the gateway to formal services. In their outreach efforts providers should recognize that shame and the desire to maintain privacy is a driving force behind the lack of disclosure. These efforts need to recognize the experience of shame and discourage self-blame and stigmatization, which hamper help-seeking efforts.

Some of the results also challenge the assumptions about why Latino women do not seek help. For example, immigration status was not associated with help-seeking, which in the field has been assumed to be an impairment in obtaining services. It is likely that undocumented legal status may be more likely to prevent disclosure to formal outlets. In contrast, cultural values, psychological reactions (e.g., shame), and acculturation are more likely to play a role in women's willingness to get help.

Future research needs to continue to expand the study of interpersonal violence beyond sexual assault and partner violence, incorporating other forms of victimization such as stalking, threat, and witnessed violence. In addition, help-seeking efforts need to be more finely evaluated to better understand their connection to mental health outcomes. Additionally, other segments of the Latino community need to be studied. For example, there is a dearth of research on victimization among Latino males and how they are impacted. Studying children and adolescents can contribute to an understanding of the developmental trajectories associated with victimization and interpersonal violence. While SALAS contributes to the body of knowledge on victimization among Latinos, there are many future opportunities for study that can further our understanding of these problems among this largest growing ethnic group.

I. INTRODUCTION

Statement of the Problem

As of 2004, Latinos constituted 14% of the United States population - the largest

minority group. Over a four-year period the number of Latinos increased 14% while the non-

Hispanic population increased by almost 2% (Pew Research Center, 2005). The large numbers

and rapid growth of this population underscore the need to focus sexual violence studies on

Latino women.

While the violence against women literature is substantial, not much research focuses on

Latino women. National surveys that evaluate victimization among women typically have a

proportion of their sample composed of Latinos (e.g., National Violence Against Women Study

[NVAW]). However, these studies do not allow for the evaluation of culturally relevant

variables that may play a role in victimization, help-seeking, or psychological outcomes. Some

of the variables that have been reported in the literature that may be of importance include

whether the individual immigrated to the United States, degree of acculturation, gender roles,

and religiosity. Another limitation of the existent Latino victimization literature is that most

samples are either small or geographically limited (e.g., restricted to a particular urban area)

which hampers the generalizability of the study results.

While the problem of sexual violence merits substantial attention, the research focusing

on Latino women typically does not address other forms of victimization. As will be evident in

our review of the literature, the victimization literature that has focused on Latino women

typically examines sexual violence or physical violence by intimates. Not addressing other co-

existing forms of victimization can result in an overestimation of the impact of a single form of victimization. Furthermore, without evaluating other forms of victimization, we are unable to evaluate to full spectrum of victimization that Latino women may experience.

Another key area in evaluating the role of sexual victimization in the lives of Latino women is understanding their help-seeking efforts. This includes paying particular attention to cultural factors that play a role in obtaining either formal (e.g., police, social service agencies) or informal (e.g., speaking with family or friends). Much of the research on sexual violence suggests that this is an underreported form of victimization. Furthermore, the literature indicates that social services are much less available to Latinos than to their non-Latino counterparts. As such, very few incidents of sexual assault reach the attention of authorities, and many women do not receive assistance in dealing with the negative impact of sexual violence. This is a concerning issue since well-tailored support services can play a key role in helping women overcome the negative sequelae of sexual violence. Understanding the factors that contribute to Latino women's help-seeking efforts is key in developing culturally sensitive and effective interventions to promote help-seeking and assistance for sexually victimized Latino women. Currently, there is an absence of quantitative research that helps us understand what contributes to help-seeking, which help-seeking modalities are more likely to be sought out, and what cultural factors may play a role in a woman's willingness to get assistance after sexual victimization.

The SALAS study aimed to fill a number of the gaps in the current literature by focusing on the sexual victimization experiences of Latino women. The strengths of this study include (1) an examination of many forms of sexual victimization including childhood and adult victimization, (2) an analysis of the other forms of victimization sexually victimized women faced during childhood and adulthood, (3) a thorough analysis of the help-seeking efforts of

Latino women that addresses both effectiveness of services and help-seeking barriers, (4)

measurement of particular cultural factors that may effect sexually victimized Latino women,

and (5) an assessment of current psychosocial outcomes associated with victimization. The

findings address significant gaps in the literature, as well as allow for empirically informed

practice and policy implications.

Literature Citation and Review

Rates of Sexual Assault in Women

Sexual assault against women has received considerable research attention over the past

30 years with much of it focusing on the extent of the problem and the psychological impact on

victims. Research focusing on childhood sexual abuse (CSA) highlights the large scope of the

problem. Overall, incidence rates of CSA have been found to be between 1.2 to 96 per 1,000

children, with abuse against girls being up to three times higher than for boys (Finkelhor,

Hamby, Ormrod, & Turner, 2005; Sedlak & Broadhurst, 1996; U.S. Department of Health and

Human Services, 2008). The large discrepancy between these rates is primarily due to the

former figure being based on agency reports while the latter figure being based on self-report

methodology. Prevalence estimates of CSA among women range from 9% to 32% (Briere &

Elliott, 2003; Tjaden & Thoennes, 2000). Lifetime (adult and childhood) sexual victimization

rates for women range from 9% to 22% (Elliott, Mok, & Briere, 2004; Kessler, Sonnega,

Bromet, & Hughes, 1995; Koss, Gidycz, & Wisniewski, 1987; Tjaden & Thoennes, 2000)

depending on the methodology and definition of sexual victimization used.

While these results clearly indicate the large impact of this problem, studies on Latino

women have reported mixed results in the victimization rates in comparison to their non-Latino

counterparts. Statistics from the U.S. Department of Health and Human Services (U.S.

Department of Health and Human Services, 2008), show that Latino children's rate of sexual victimization was second only to that of Caucasian children. The NIS – 3 (Sedlak & Broadhurst, 1996) found no differences between Latino children and children of other races on the rate of sexual victimization. A study with adult women in a primary care setting also found no significant differences in rates of childhood sexual abuse between Latino and Caucasian women (Katerndahl, Burge, Kellogg, & Parra, 2005). In contrast, Urquiza and Goodlin-Jones (1994) found Latino adult women to report a 25% rate of childhood sexual abuse, which was almost 15% to 20% lower than the rates reported by Caucasian or African-American women. With respect to lifetime rates of rape, the NVAW study found that Latino women reported significantly lower rates (14.6%) than non-Latino women (18.4%) (Tjaden & Thoennes, 2000). It is arguable whether these conflicting reports reflect actual rates, reporting bias, methodological differences, or some combination of all of these factors. However, this mixed evidence highlights the importance of further studying sexual victimization among Latino women to gain a better understanding of the scope and impact of this problem.

Sexual Abuse and Other Forms of Victimizations

Two types of multiple victimizations - concurrent multiple types of victimization (polyvictimization) and multiple victimizations that occur over different periods, such as childhood and adulthood, of one individual type (revictimization) shed light on the extent to which sexual violence is associated with other forms of victimization.

Adult women. Various studies find substantial overlap between sexual violence and other forms of interpersonal violence. Frieze (1983) examined sexual violence among a sample of battered women and a comparison group of non-battered women. She found that over a third of the battered sample reported being raped by their husbands (34%). This was significantly higher than the rate of rape among the non-battered comparison group (1%). Additionally, battered

women who were raped by their partners reported higher levels of other victimization such as

being raped by someone other than their husbands than the non-raped battered women. Campbell

and Soeken (1999) asked a volunteer community sample of battered women about their forced

sex experiences. Almost half the sample reported being sexually victimized and these

participants were assessed to be in significantly more danger, have experienced more physical

and non-physical abuse, and have a greater number of health problems. These studies are

supported by more recent research that finds that Latino women often experience multiple forms

of victimization, with studies reporting that between 18% and 95% of victimized Latino women

experience more than one form of victimization (Clemmons, DiLillo, Martinez, DeGue, &

Jeffcot, 2003; Coker, Smith, Bethea, King, & McKeown, 2000; Hass, Dutton, & Orloff, 2000).

This research supports the notion that sexually victimized Latino women are likely to be

experiencing other forms of victimization in addition to sexual violence.

   With respect to revictimization, women who are sexually victimized in adulthood are

likely to have been victims of sexual violence during childhood. Elliott, Mok and Briere (2004)

found that child sexual abuse and childhood physical abuse were unique predictors of adult

sexual abuse among a nationally representative sample. Briere and Elliot (2003), using a

geographically stratified national sample, also found that those who had been victimized as

children had higher rates of victimization as adults. A review of empirical literature showed that

two of three individuals who experienced sexual victimization are revictimized later in their lives

(Classen, et al., 2005) with some studies finding a three-fold increase in revictimization risk for

sexually victimized women (Arata, 2002; Desai, Arias, Thomson, & Basile, 2002). In addition,

other types of childhood victimization, such as neglect and emotional abuse, are also linked with adult trauma in general (Spertus, Yehuda, Wong, Halligan, & Seremetis, 2003). Thus, revictimization can be examined both with-in types of victimization (e.g., child sexual and adult sexual) and across victimization types (e.g., child sexual and adult physical).

Children. Finkelhor and colleagues (2005) assessed a broad spectrum of victimizations among youth in their Developmental Victimization Survey. A nationally representative sample of youth ages 2 to 17 ($N = 2,030$) was asked about 34 forms of offenses in five general areas: conventional crime, child maltreatment, peer and sibling victimization, sexual assault, and witnessing and indirect victimization. Among those who were sexually victimized, 97% were also victimized in some other way. Eighty-two percent of those sexually victimized also reported assault, whereas 84% reported witnessing or experiencing indirect violence. This was the highest percent of overlap among victimization types assessed. Children who reported completed rape reported an average of 7.6 kinds of victimizations, which included other forms of maltreatment, peer/sibling violence, and conventional forms of crime. These findings show that sexually abused children are at particular risk for other forms of victimizations.

In a subsequent analysis employing the same dataset, sexually victimized youth were most likely to be represented among polyvictims, those who experienced multiple types of victimization during childhood (Finkelhor, et al., 2007a). Polyvictimized children reported more trauma symptomatology than children who were not polyvictimized and children who experienced repeated episodes of the same type of victimization (see Trickett, 1998 for similar findings). Most importantly, the results show that including polyvictimization as a predictor of outcomes dwarfed the influence of individual types of victimization. These findings caution researchers that including individual victimization types to the exclusion of polyvictimization might lead to false conclusions about the importance of a particular type of victimization.

Finkelhor, Ormrod and Turner (2007b) successfully contacted 79.5% of the above nationally representative sample one year later and assessed further victimization. The resultant odds ratio for re-victimization was 10.6 for sexual revictimization and 10.0 for child maltreatment - the two highest odds ratios for victimization types. Additionally, the odds ratio for being characterized as polyvictimized, if the participant was polyvictimized at Time 1 was 8.7. Further, any type of victimization was associated with increased risk for other kinds of victimizations. Boney-McCoy & Finkelhor (1995) found similar results with multiple types of victimization surfacing as a predictor of subsequent CSA and prior sexual abuse as an especially strong predictor of later CSA. These findings underscore the extreme risk of revictimization among sexually victimized and polyvictimized youth.

Latino women. A smaller set of studies has examined polyvictimization and revictimization among Latino women. McFarlane et al. (1998) recruited a sample of 329 pregnant Latino women who sought prenatal care. Approximately a third of the sample experienced sexual violence during the 12 months prior to the interview. Comparisons between sexually victimized and non-sexually victimized Latino women show that those who were sexually victimized reported significantly higher levels of threats of abuse and physical abuse. For sexually victimized women there was a correlation of .42 between physical abuse and sexual abuse. In another study, 243 racially diverse college students reported on childhood sexual abuse and adult rape (Urquiza & Goodlin-Jones, 1994). Twenty-five percent of Latino women reported CSA and 18% of Latino women reported rape. For all ethnic/racial groups combined, women with a history of CSA were three times more likely to be raped in adulthood. However, among Latino women, those who experienced CSA were four times as likely to report rape in adulthood. The authors posit that cultural factors influence risk factors for revictimization. These studies suggest that revictimization and polyvictimization rates may vary by ethnic/racial group and point to the importance of culturally relevant factors that may help explain these differing rates.

Service Utilization

Currently, there are few research articles on the help-seeking behavior of Latino women who have been sexually abused. This is an important research question that needs to be addressed in order to develop prevention and intervention efforts. Research on the help-seeking associated with intimate partner violence and sexual abuse among the general population provides insight on the help-seeking efforts of Latino women.

Help-seeking. Victimized women rely on formal and informal help-seeking. Formal avenues include police, the criminal justice system, and mental health professionals whereas informal avenues include friends and relatives. A recent theoretical framework put forth by Liang et al. (2005) conceptualizes help-seeking as a process including defining the problem, deciding to seek help, and selecting a source of support. Each of these stages is influenced by individual, interpersonal, and sociocultural factors. Some of the sociocultural factors that are relevant to a discussion of Latino women include cultural norms sanctioning violence, fewer material resources and a lack of culturally-sensitive services. These barriers are often present for marginalized groups and are exacerbated among immigrants. Latina immigrants might face problems such as lack of information, poor familiarity with the social service system, social isolation, poor English language skills, and fear of deportation (Adames & Campbell, 2005; Raj & Silverman, 2002). This contextual analysis of help-seeking behavior is vital to understanding Latino women's efforts to manage victimization (see Dutton, 1996).

In general, Latino women do not rely on help sources at the same rate as Anglo-Americans. A study on the mental health and medical services sought by sexually victimized women found that sexual assault was associated with both types of services. Latinos in the study were less likely to seek services than non-Latino whites (Golding, et al., 1988). A study using a nationally representative sample found that Latino ethnic identity was associated with significantly less formal help-seeking (Lewis, et al., 2005). In addition, this study also found that sexual assault was associated with more informal and formal help-seeking, with seeking help from friends being the most common behavior for the entire sample (Lewis, et al., 2005). West et al. (1998) found that battered Latino women seek less formal and informal help than Anglo battered women. Latino women who sought help were more likely to be acculturated, as evidenced by an English language preference, than Latino women who did not seek help. Another source of hesitancy on the part of Latino women to seek formal assistance may be a result of perceived practical barriers that prevent them from seeking help, including financial dependence on their husbands, fear of deportation, and lack of insurance (Bauer, Rodriguez, Quiroga, & Flores-Ortiz, 2000; Cabassa, Zayas, & Hansen, 2006; Lipsky & Caetano, 2007; Torres & Campbell, 1998). Recent research has provided further support around the fear of deportation, since immigrant Latino women are less likely to seek out formal agency services (Ingram, 2007).

Another factor that plays a role in diminished help-seeking by Latinos is the lack of available mental health services for Latinos (Cabassa, et al., 2006; U.S. Department of Health and Human Services, 2001). A principal culprit for this problem is the lack of services in Spanish, given that approximately 40% of Latinos in the United States report not speaking English "very well" (Ramirez, 2004). Lack of linguistically sensitive providers is supported by research which has found that the ratio of mental health professionals to population for Latinos was 29 per 100,000 compared to 173 per 100,000 for Caucasians (U.S. Department of Health and Human Services, 2001). These data demonstrate that the availability of providers for Latinos is less than 1/5th of what is available to the English-speaking population. In addition to this evidence, a recent qualitative study by Barrio and colleagues (Barrio, et al., 2008) highlights the perception, by both service providers and consumers, that Latinos have neither sufficient available resources nor adequate information on available mental health services. The current study will add substantially to the understanding of help-seeking among sexually victimized Latino women. Questions will be targeted to understand which services sexually victimized Latino women sought, how useful those services were, and reasons for not seeking particular services. This data interpreted in light of victimization experiences (e.g., perpetrator, age of victimization, severity, chronicity), immigration status, and cultural factors such as religiosity, gender role ideology, and acculturation will offer insightful findings for research, practice, and policy.

Culturally-Relevant Factors

Acculturation level, gender role ideology, and religiosity are constructs relevant to the help-seeking decisions of victimized Latino women. These factors may influence the reporting of interpersonal violence, the psychological impact of victimization, and help-seeking efforts. Prior research has not assessed how these factors are linked with sexual victimization among Latino women.

Religiosity. Religion refers to "a fixed system of ideals or ideological commitments (p. 64)," that is separate from personal ideology, and is usually formal and institutional. Spirituality, on the other hand, refers more to the personal, subjective side of religiosity and is usually unsystematic, emotional, and inward. Both religion and spirituality are linked with positive mental and physical health outcomes (Hill & Pargament, 2003).

Comas-Diaz (1995) suggests that religious beliefs might play a negative role in coping with child sexual abuse among Puerto Ricans and that such beliefs must be included in treatment plans. The culturally embedded concept of fatalism, a belief that events are under God's control and not personal control, might direct victims to endure suffering, try to portray self-control, or alternatively, avoid facing the problem (Comas-Diaz & Fontes, 1995). Research has yet to test these assumptions and whether this link exists between religiosity and sexual victimization experiences.

Acculturation and gender role ideology. Acculturation refers to the social and psychological changes (i.e., attitudes, behavior, values, and sense of cultural identity) that take place when minority members come in contact with the dominant culture (Cabassa, 2003). Current conceptualizations of the acculturation process include two dimensions - adherence to the dominant culture and maintenance of the culture of origin - resulting in four acculturation strategies (assimilation, separation, integration and marginalization) (Cabassa, 2003; Phinney & Flores, 2002). As Latino women become more involved with the dominant American culture, traditional sex role attitudes are weakened (Phinney & Flores, 2002).

The relationship between acculturation, the related change in gender roles (Phinney & Flores, 2002; Valentine & Mosley, 2000), and victimization is not clearly understood. Two hypotheses seem plausible. The stress associated with acculturation, particularly change in gender roles, can increase the likelihood of abuse (Adames & Campbell, 2005). Alternatively, lack of acculturation may involve low educational attainment and occupational choices, and poor understanding of the social service system, placing Latinas at risk for victimization.

Traditional gender roles in the Latino community are exemplified through the concepts of marianismo and machismo. These gendered scripts are hypothesized to play an important role in victimization and responses to victimization (Comas-Diaz & Fontes, 1995; Perilla, Bakerman, & Norris, 1994; Vasquez, 1998). According to the concept of marianismo, based on the Virgin Mary, women are supposed to be submissive and self-sacrificing. Machismo includes honor, pride, courage, aggressive behavior, and domination. This dominance/submission dynamic influences interactions in Latino families and may change during the acculturation process.

There is preliminary evidence to support the hypothesis that acculturation to the American dominant culture and non-traditional gender roles increases victimization among Latino women. Harris et al. (2005) found that among a sample of Latino women, traditional gender role attitudes were associated with less reported physical abuse. Acculturation was also found to be associated with more reported intimate partner violence (Garcia, Hurwitz, & Kraus, 2004). Alternatively, acculturation may also be associated with a greater willingness to report victimization. Kaufman Kantor et al. (1994) found that being born in the U.S., which was highly correlated with acculturation, was associated with higher levels of physical assault in intimate relationships. Similar results were found by Sorenson and Telles (1991): Mexican Americans born in the U.S. reported rates of intimate partner violence (IPV) 2.4 times higher than those born in Mexico. Woman's financial contribution had a positive effect on rates of IPV (Perilla, Bakerman, & Norris, 1994). Women contributing to the financial maintenance of a family might represent a divergence from traditional gender roles and a challenge to machismo. Additionally, a qualitative study looked at immigrant Latinas' understanding of intimate partner violence (Adames & Campbell, 2005). Participants often cited external forces such as traditional gender roles and acculturation stress as causes of IPV. Research has not yet examined the relationship between gender role ideology, acculturation, and sexual victimization. This study will address the current gap in the literature by including these constructs.

Psychosocial Impact of Sexual Violence

Research has shown that victims of CSA experience significant psychological distress and psychopathology (Briere & Elliott, 2003; Browne & Finkelhor, 1986; Finkelhor, et al., 1990; Kendall-Tackett, Williams, & Finkelhor, 1993; Neumann, et al., 1996). Some of the more commonly reported problems include Posttraumatic Stress Disorder (PTSD), depression, anxiety, anger problems, pathological dissociation, fearfulness, substance abuse, self-injurious behavior and suicidality, and sexual problems (Anderson, et al., 1993; Briere & Conte, 1993; Briere, Woo, McRae, Foltz, & Sitzman, 1997; Briggs, 1997; Browne & Finkelhor, 1986; Callahan, 2003; Gorcey, Santiago, & McCall-Perez, 1986; Heath, Bean, & Feinauer, 1996; Merrill, Guimond, Thomsen, & Milner, 2003; Neumann, et al., 1996; Nishith, et al., 2000; Romano & De Luca, 2001; Tyler, 2002; Wolfe, 1994; Wyatt, Guthrie, & Notgrass, 1992).

Research on sexual violence has also found that CSA is a risk factor for adult victimization, indicating that women abused as children are at risk for later victimization in adulthood (Briere & Elliott, 2003; Classen, et al., 2005; Nishith, et al., 2000; Urquiza & Goodlin-Jones, 1994; Wyatt, et al., 1992). This consequence of sexual violence confounds the impact of sexual assault and rape in adulthood since many of these women may be victims of multiple incidents of sexual victimization, which has been shown to increase reported psychological distress (Banyard, et al., 2001; Nishith, et al., 2000). Keeping this issue in mind, research on the psychological sequelae of sexual victimization in adulthood found that the psychological distress women experience is similar to that of CSA victims. Research has found elevated rates of depression, anxiety, PTSD, dissociation, avoidance, and sexual problems for women who were sexually assaulted or raped as adults (Elliott, et al., 2004), even in studies where CSA history is taken into account (Banyard, et al., 2001; Nishith, et al., 2000).

Polyvictimization and revictimization are also linked with poor psychological outcomes. Kessler et al. (1995), employing a nationally representative sample, found that women tended to report more rape, sexual molestation, childhood neglect, and childhood physical abuse than men and were more likely to develop PTSD. Moreover, women who experience multiple forms of abuse are likely to have more devastating psychological outcomes. CDC researchers (Basile, Arias, Desai, & Thompson, 2004) examined the effect of multiple forms of abuse by computing a dose variable which took into account the number and severity of types of intimate partner violence. The dose variable solely accounted for 32% of the variation in PTSD symptomatology.

The research on the psychosocial impact of sexual violence for Latino women has not received as much attention. However, the results appear to be consistent with respect to the impact of CSA and adult sexual violence on Latino women. Latino women tend to experience the same types of symptomatology described above with most studies finding levels similar to those of other ethnic groups (Mennen, 1995; Vasquez, 1998). Sander-Phillips and colleagues' (1995) study is one of the exceptions in that it found higher elevations of depression among Latino women compared to African-American and Caucasian women. These findings raise questions about comparisons within different Latino groups, and cultural factors that may influence the relationship between victimization and psychological distress. In addition, research needs to address less-often studied types of symptomatology (e.g., dissociation, sexual problems) and their relationship to victimization in Latino women.

Summary of Prior Research

Prior research confirms that a significant percentage of women are sexually victimized in childhood and adulthood. However, research shows mixed results in the victimization rates of Latino women compared with non-Latinos. In addition, the literature shows considerable overlap among abuse types as well as the link between childhood sexual victimization and adult victimization. Studies on polyvictimization and revictimization show that focusing on one victimization type at one point in time can only capture a very limited set of experiences. However, research with Latinos has primarily focused on either sexual assault or physical violence by an intimate partner only, ignoring other forms of abuse and victimization. This study examined sexual victimization, in addition to physical assault (e.g., childhood physical abuse, intimate partner violence), witnessing and indirect violence, and stalking, aiming to overcome some of the prior limitations in this line of research.

There is currently limited research examining service utilization among sexually victimized Latino women. Our study examines the rate of help-seeking from informal and formal sources, satisfaction level of these services, and their perceived effectiveness. Additionally, help-seeking efforts are analyzed taking into consideration victimization history, immigration status, and other demographic factors. This information aims to benefit service providers and provide guidance about potential outreach and education services. Additionally, since little is known about how religiosity, acculturation, and gender role ideology impact experience, responses, and outcomes associated with sexual victimization, we are able to conduct a culturally-relevant examination of the issues at hand and add to a more complete understanding of the role of cultural factors on victimization among Latino women.

Finally, research unambiguously shows poor psychosocial outcomes associated with sexual victimization. Whereas these effects are expected to hold for Latino women, our study allows for a more nuanced analysis of these issues. We examine how childhood sexual victimization, adult sexual victimization, revictimization, and polyvictimization are linked with psychosocial outcomes.

Statement of Hypotheses/Research Rationale

Given the presented literature, we pose the following hypotheses for our study goals.

Goal 1: Determine extent of sexual victimization in a sample of adult Latino females.

Objective 1: Determine the rate of attempted sexual assault, sexual assault and rape experienced in childhood.

Objective 2: Determine the rate of attempted sexual assault, sexual assault and rape experienced in adulthood.

Goal 2: Determine the coexistence of other forms of victimization among those sexually victimized and the risk for subsequent victimization.

Objective 1: Determine rate of physical assaults during childhood and adulthood among sexually victimized Latino women (e.g., IPV, childhood physical abuse).

Objective 2: Determine rate of witnessed and indirect victimization during childhood and adulthood among sexually victimized Latino women.

Objective 3: Determine the extent of stalking victimization among sexually victimized Latino women.

Objective 4: Determine the extent that sexual victimization is a risk factor for subsequent victimization in Latino women.

Objective 5: Determine the percentage of participants who experienced multiple forms of victimization (i.e., sexual, physical, indirect, and stalking).

Goal 3: Examine formal service utilization among sexually victimized Latino women.

Objective 1: Determine rate and factors associated with reporting victimization to police.

Objective 2: Determine rate and factors associated with using legal remedies.

Objective 3: Determine rate and factors associated with the use of therapeutic services.

Objective 4: Determine rate and factors associated with the use of medical services.

Objective 5: Determine rate and factors associated with seeking religious counsel.

Objective 6: Determine the relationship between victimization experiences and formal help-seeking.

Objective 7: Determine satisfaction with above services and its relationship with psychosocial outcomes.

Goal 4: Examine informal help-seeking among sexually victimized Latino women.

Objective 1: Determine rate and factors associated with disclosure to and support from friends/peers and how helpful participants found this support to be.

Objective 2: Determine rate and factors associated with disclosure to and support from family and how helpful participants found this support to be.

Goal 5: Examine culturally-relevant factors associated with experience and responses to sexual violence.

Objective 1: Examine the influence of religiosity on the impact and response to sexual victimization.

Objective 2: Examine the influence of acculturation on the impact and response to sexual victimization.

Objective 3: Examine the influence of gender role ideology on the impact and response to sexual victimization.

Goal 6: Determine the psychosocial impact of sexual victimization on Latino women.

Objective 1: Examine the relationship between different forms of sexual victimization, polyvictimization, revictimization and psychological distress (e.g., depression, anxiety, PTSD).

Objective 2: Examine the relationship between different forms of sexual victimization, polyvictimization, revictimization and social functioning (e.g., employment, educational attainment).

II. METHODS

Participants

The SALAS study assessed the victimization experiences of a national sample of 2,000 Latino women living in the United States. Trained professionals from an experienced survey research firm conducted the interviews over the phone in either English or Spanish, from May through September 2008.

The study entrance criteria were that participants needed to be women over the age of 18 who self-identified as Latino (either foreign or U.S. born), and whose primary language was either English or Spanish. The total sample consisted of 2,000 participants with the majority of participants (90%) living in high-density Latino areas (80% or higher) based on U.S. Census data. The minimum response rate (i.e., ratio of completed and screen out interviews to complete, screen-outs, partial interviews, refusals, break-offs, and no contact) for the sample was 30.7% while the minimum cooperation rate (i.e., ratio of completed and screen out interviews to complete, screen-outs, partial interviews, refusals, and break-offs) was 53.7%. The refusal rate (i.e., ratio of refusal or break-offs to completes, screen-outs, partial interviews, refusals, break-offs, no contact, other, unknown household, and unknown other) for the sample was 20.8%. The SRBI methods report (see Appendix) provides detailed response rate calculation formulas and density area data. These response rates formulas are based on standard definitions established by the American Association for Public Opinion Research (American Association for Public Opinion Research, 2009).

The average age of the participants was 47.76 years of age. Approximately 63% of the sample has a high school education or less. The majority of participants (61%) were U.S. citizens (either U.S. born or naturalized) with a small proportion of the sample not reporting any legal status category (we refer to this group as undocumented; 4.7%). Although 76.5% of the sample indicated that their preferred language was Spanish, 71.5% of the sample conducted the interview in Spanish. Approximately 56% of the participants were married, with the smallest percentages for cohabitating (7.6%), divorced (10.1%), and widowed (10.1). Detailed sample demographics are presented in Table 1.

Table 1

Sample Descriptives (N = 2,000)

	Mean/*n*	SD/%	Range
Age	47.76	16.24	18 – 95
18 – 24	143	7.2	
25 – 34	328	16.5	
35 – 44	428	21.5	
45 – 54	389	19.6	
55 – 64	341	17.2	
65+	358	18.0	
	n	%	
Education Level			
Less that high school	760	38.3	
High school grad/GED	495	24.9	
Some college/trade school	278	14.0	

Two year college graduate	137	6.9
Four year college graduate	205	10.3
Some graduate school	25	1.3
Graduate degree	84	4.2
Immigration Status		
U.S. born citizen	549	28.5
Naturalized citizen	628	32.6
Permanent resident	533	27.7
Current visa	80	4.2
Refugee/asylum	2	0.1
Awaiting status	44	2.3
None of the above/ Undocumented	91	4.7
Preferred Language		
English	379	19.1
Spanish	1,518	76.4
Both Spanish and English	87	4.4
Other	3	0.2
Interview Language		
English	570	28.5
Spanish	1,429	71.5
Relationship Status		
Single (never married)	261	13.2
Married	1,115	56.3

Cohabitating/committed relationship	151	7.6
Divorced	199	10.1
Widowed	200	10.1
Other	54	2.7
Employment Status		
Employed full-time	548	27.7
Employed part-time	217	11.0
Unemployed	197	9.9
Retired	250	12.6
Homemaker	585	29.6
Other (students, public assistance, etc)	181	9.1
Household Income		
Under $9,999	367	26.1
$10,000 – $19,999	366	26.0
$20,000 – $29,999	229	16.3
$30,000 – $39,999	133	9.4
$40,000 – $49,999	95	6.7
$50,000 – $59,999	57	4.0
$60,000 – $69,999	39	2.8
$70,000 – $79,999	30	2.1
$80,000 or more	92	6.5
Sexual Orientation		
Straight/Heterosexual	1,926	98.7

Lesbian	13	0.7
Bisexual	13	0.7

The participants in the sample were predominantly immigrants from Mexico or of Mexican descent (67.1% and 89.5% respectively), with the second most common immigrant group being from Cuba (18%). Detailed ethnicity data are presented in Table 2. The regional distribution, presented in Table 3, shows that 50% of the sample was from Texas, with 25.2% being from California, 20.4% being from Florida, and the remaining 4.6% being from 12 other states.

In comparing our sample to available U.S. Census figures on Latinos, we have a notably higher median age (median age for U.S. Latino women is 26.3 years versus 47.0 median age for the SALAS sample). Our sample has a higher rate of a high school education and beyond, a similar proportion of being married, and a smaller proportion of being born in the U.S. or being U.S. citizens (Guzman, 2001; Ramirez, 2004; U.S. Census Bureau, 2000). In evaluating ethnic background, the SALAS sample has a larger proportion of individuals of Mexican and Cuban descent (U.S. Census Bureau, 2000). These demographic discrepancies may be in part influenced by our methodology and screening procedures. Since our study focused on adult women, there were no participants under the age of 18. In addition, RDD methodology only calls landline phones, given the growth of mobile phones, it is possible that younger individuals and those of lower socioeconomic status may have been under-sampled (Blumberg & Luke, 2009).

Table 2

Ethnicity and Country of Origin Descriptives

	U.S. Born (*n* = 533)		Immigrant (*n* = 1,439)	
	n	%	*n*	%
Mexico	477	89.5	966	67.1
Cuba	16	3.0	259	18.0
Puerto Rico	14	2.6	16	1.1
Dominican Republic	1	0.0	15	1.0
Other	25	4.7	183	12.7

Table 3

Sample Regional Distribution

State	*n*	%
Texas	999	50.0
California	503	25.2
Florida	408	20.4
Arizona	42	2.1
New Mexico	22	1.1
Other[a]	27	1.4

[a] Includes CT, ID, IL, MD, MA, NV, NJ, NY, PA, WV

Measures

The SRBI methods report (see Appendix) provides a complete version of the survey, as it was programmed into the CATI software, which presents all the survey questions, response choices, and skip patterns for the interview.

Demographic Information. Participant background information was asked on personal characteristics including age, country of origin, immigration status, preferred language, sexual orientation, educational level, employment status, household income, housing status, and relationship status. Regional information was obtained from the census tract information linked to the random digit dialing (RDD) blocks.

State of Social Issues Questionnaire (SSIQ). The SSIQ were questions developed specifically for this survey to evaluate the participants' view of how much of a problem discrimination, violent crime, domestic violence, sexual assault and sexual harassment were in society today. The 11 questions asked about how much these issues were a problem generally in society and how much they were a problem for Latinos in particular. Each item asks to what degree each issue is a problem on a 5-point Likert scale ranging from 1 (Not at all) to 5 (Very big).

Lifetime Trauma and Victimization History (LTVH). The LTVH evaluates lifetime trauma and victimization history in reference to 30 various traumatic experiences (Widom, et al., 2005). The full version of the LTVH includes questions about natural disasters, combat experience, property loss, interpersonal violence, and witnessed victimization. As the focus of this study was on interpersonal victimization, we limited LTVH questions to stalking, physical assaults, weapon assaults, physical assaults in childhood, threats, threats with weapons, sexual assault, attempted sexual assault, sexual fondling, kidnapping, and witnessed victimization.

44

Each affirmative incident on the LTVH was followed-up with questions regarding the age of occurrence, duration, frequency, perpetrator, injury, and posttraumatic reaction (i.e., being in danger of death or serious injury and experiencing intense fear, helplessness, or horror). For perpetrator data participants were asked an open-ended question of "who did this to you", their response was then categorized into one of the possible response choices (see Appendix pg. 38) which were then condensed into the descriptive categories presented which include parents, other relatives, a partner/spouse/dating relationship, siblings, other known perpetrator, stranger, or multiple perpetrators. For our presented categories "multiple" refers to multiple perpetrators for the same assault incident (e.g., gang rape). Furthermore, due to the ethnic background of the study participants and the focus on help-seeking, a question was asked as to whether each incident took place while the participant lived in the United States. For each affirmative incident type, respondents were asked if anyone else ever did that to them. If so, respondents completed a second loop with regard to the incident type. Due to time constraints in the survey, only the follow-up questions of age of occurrence and number of times was asked for witnessed violence questions with no second loops being asked. The victimization incidents were then consolidated into five categories: Physical assaults, sexual assaults, stalking, threat victimization, and witnessed victimization. This was also divided by whether the victimization events took place in childhood (defined as occurring prior to age 18) or adulthood. This categorization is presented in Table 4. The calculation of each victimization category across developmental period (childhood or adulthood) was calculated by using the age when victimization experience first and last took place. However, in the regression models, the total victimization variable was simply a count of the interpersonal victimization screener questions, excluding witnessed violence. A copy of the version of the LTVH as was administered in the interview is included in the SRBI methods

report in the Appendix.

Table 4

Screener Question Categories

Screener Question	Recoded Category
1. Have you ever been *stalked* by anyone? For example, has anyone ever followed or spied on you?	Stalking
2. Have you ever been *shot at, stabbed, struck, kicked, beaten, punched, slapped around, or otherwise physically harmed*?	Physical Assault
3. Have you ever been *threatened with any kind of a weapon*, like a knife, gun, baseball bat, frying pan, scissors, stick, rock or bottle?	Threat Victimization
4. Has anyone ever *threatened* you in a face-to-face confrontation?	Threat Victimization
5. Have you ever been *actually assaulted with any kind of a weapon*, like a knife, gun, baseball bat, frying pan, scissors, stick, rock, or bottle?	Physical Assault
6. When you were a child--that is, when you were in elementary or middle school, before about age 12--were you ever *struck, kicked, beaten, punched, slapped around, spanked hard enough to leave a mark, or otherwise physically harmed*?	Physical Assault
7. Deleted	Removed from protocol
8. Has anyone--male or female--ever forced or coerced you to engage in unwanted sexual activity? By unwanted sexual activity, I mean vaginal, oral, or anal intercourse, or has anyone inserted an object or their fingers in your anus or vagina?	Sexual Assault
9. Other than what we just talked about, did anyone, male or female ever *attempt to--but not actually--* force you to engage in unwanted sexual activity?	Sexual Assault
10. Other than what we just talked about, has anyone ever *actually* touched private parts of your body or made you touch theirs against your wishes?	Sexual Assault

11. Have you ever been kidnapped or held captive?	Excluded due to low N
12. Have you ever been in any OTHER situation in which you were in danger of death or serious physical injury, or in which you felt intense fear, helplessness or horror?	Coded depending on response
13. Have you ever seen or been present when someone was murdered or seriously injured?	Witnessed Victimization
14. Have you ever seen or been present when *another person* was shot at, stabbed, struck, kicked, beaten, slapped around, or otherwise physically harmed?	Witnessed Victimization
15. Have you ever seen or been present when another person was raped, sexually attacked, or made to engage in unwanted sexual activity? By unwanted sexual activity, we mean vaginal, oral, or anal intercourse; insertion of an object or fingers in the anus or vagina; having private parts of their body touched or being made to touch other's private parts against their wishes?	Witnessed Victimization
16. Have you ever *lived in a war zone?* (For example, lived in an area with guerilla warfare).	Excluded due to low N and not being interpersonal in nature (included for exploratory purposes in this sample)

Help-Seeking Questionnaire (HSQ). The help-seeking questionnaire was developed specifically for this study but was formed from two large scale studies that assessed formal and informal help-seeking behaviors (Block, 2000; Gelles & Straus, 1988). This questionnaire asked about the actions taken by respondents after experiencing an identified incident of victimization. Participants chose the anchor incident by identifying the "most severe incident that occurred in the United States and has upset you the most" for any direct form of victimization (i.e., they could not report help-seeking on any witnessed violence). Questions included information about the various types of resources, both formal and informal, that participants may have contacted for assistance such as police, the courts, social service agencies, medical care, family, friends, and clergy. Participants were also asked about the effectiveness and satisfaction level with the utilized services. Open-ended questions queried participants who did not use each resource as to why they refrained from seeking help.

Brief Multidimensional Measure of Religiousness/Spirituality (BMMRS). The BMMRS is a 33-item multidimensional measure that examines religiousness and spirituality designed for health-related studies. The questions cover topics such as religious affiliation, personal religious/spiritual history, public religious practices, private religious practices, social support, religious coping, beliefs and values, commitment, forgiveness, daily spiritual experiences, and overall self-ranking. This study only used the congregation support, positive religious coping, negative religious coping, and religious intensity indices along one item from the beliefs and values index. As the positive and negative religious coping subscales constitute the RCOPE, that is also embedded in our questionnaire (Pargament, et al., 2000). Participants responded to each statement on a scale of 1 (a great deal) to 4 (not at all). Psychometric evaluation, reported from use of the instrument in the General Social Survey (Idler, et al., 2003), has found the pertinent indices to have internal consistency coefficients (alphas) ranging from .54 to .86 (Idler, et al., 2003). In our victimized subsample the internal consistency coefficients (alphas) were .47 for Religious Support, .77 for Positive Religious Coping, and .50 for Negative Religious Coping.

Brief Acculturation Rating Scale of Mexican-Americans – II (Brief ARSMA – II). The Brief ARSMA-II assesses both minority and majority cultural identity (Bauman, 2005) and includes items from the complete ARSMA-II (Cuellar, Arnold, & Maldonado, 1995). Participants report the degree to which each statement accurately describes them on a scale of 1 (not at all) to 5 (almost always). The scale is often used with the Latino population in general (Cuellar, et al., 1995) and none of the items refer to Mexican culture in particular. A reported alpha coefficient for the Mexican orientation scale was .91 and .73 for the Anglo oriented scale on a sample of middle school and elementary school students. Acculturation score also significantly correlated to language chosen to respond to the scale. For our sample, we found high internal consistency (alpha) for both the Anglo orientation scale (.78) and Mexican orientation scale (.86).

Short Bem Sex Role Inventory (BSRI- Short Form). This instrument measures sex-typed personality characteristics by asking participants to report the degree to which each of 30 adjectives describes them. The instrument consists of 30 adjectives - 10 masculine, 10 feminine and 10 neutral items (Beere, 1990; Bem, 1981). The BSRI is the most commonly used instrument in gender-related research, has been used with minority groups, and was normed in the United States (Beere, 1990). The Femininity and Masculinity scales are a calculation of the mean score for the items on those scales. Both the Masculinity and Femininity scales aim to measure the degree to which someone conforms to the culturally defined sex-appropriate behavior for that sex role (Bem, 1981). Femininity items include adjectives such as "affectionate", "compassionate", and "gentle". Masculinity items include adjectives such as "aggressive", "assertive", and "dominant". For this survey, the standard 7-point Likert-type scale was abbreviated to a 5-point Likert-type scale for easier phone administration. Both the Masculine (.80) and Feminine (.87) scales had strong reliability coefficients (alpha) in our victimized subsample.

Trauma Symptom Inventory (TSI). The TSI is a 100-item instrument that evaluates posttraumatic and trauma related symptomatology in adults. The TSI consists of 3 validity scales and 10 clinical scales (Briere, 1995). Each item asks about the frequency of occurrence of each symptom on a 4-point Likert scale ranging from 0 (never) to 3 (often). The TSI has been normed with men or women over the age of 18. For the purposes of this study only the Anxious Arousal, Depression, Anger/Irritability, and Dissociation scales were used. These scales have been found to have excellent reliability, with alphas ranging between .82 (Dissociation) and .91 (Depression) (Briere, 1995, 1996). Reliability (Cronbach's alpha) of the TSI scales for our sample was: .86 for Anxious Arousal, .86 for Depression, .89 for Anger/Irritability, and .86 for Dissociation. Validity has also been supported for the TSI across various samples (Briere, 1995, 1996; McDevitt-Murphy, Weathers, & Adkins, 2005).

PTSD Checklist (PCL). The PCL is a 17-item instrument for assessing the severity of PTSD symptomatology (Weathers, et al., 1993). Participants are asked how much they have been bothered by each symptom in the past month, with responses being rated on a 5-point Likert scale ranging from 1 (not at all) to 5 (extremely). This measure covers the three main symptom clusters of the DSM-IV criteria for PTSD: reexperiencing, numbing/avoidance, and hyperarousal (American Psychiatric Association, 2000). The PCL has shown excellent reliability, with alpha coefficients regularly above .90 (Blanchard, Jones-Alexander, Buckley, & Forneris, 1996; Buckley, Blanchard, & Hickling, 1996; Cuevas, et al., 2006; Weathers, et al., 1993). This instrument has also demonstrated excellent diagnostic utility (.79 to .90) against "gold standard" measures of PTSD using varying cut scores (between 30 and 50) with different populations (Andrykowski & Cordova, 1998; Andrykowski, Cordova, Studts, & Miller, 1998; Blanchard, Jones-Alexander, Buckley, & Forneris, 1996; Bollinger, Cuevas, Vielhauer, Morgan, & Keane, 2008; Manne, Du Hamel, Gallelli, Sorgen, & Redd, 1998). The PCL has an existing Spanish version with comparable psychometric properties (Marshall, 2004; Marshall & Orlando, 2002). Reliability (Cronbach's alpha) for our victimized subsample was .93.

Procedures

Probability samples of households with telephones were generated using a random digit dial method (RDD). In this kind of sample, a listing is constructed of all one hundred-block numbers, or the first eight digits of a ten digit phone number to which residential numbers are assigned. A random sample of these hundred blocks was drawn. For SALAS, the sample was arranged based on the Latino density for the hundred blocks. Next, two random digits were added to each hundred block prefix, thus producing a population-based, random digit dialing sample of telephone numbers stratified by Hispanic household density per hundred block. All calls were made between 5pm and 9pm during the weekdays, between 10am to 9pm on Saturdays, and 11am to 9pm on Sundays. Eligible households within the total sample were then selected. Telephone interviewing has been found to be comparable with in-person interviews in its reliability and validity (Bajos, Spira, Ducot, & Messiah, 1992; Bermack, 1989; Czaja, 1987; Martin, Duncan, Powers, & Sawyer, 1989), although as previously mentioned, it may under-sample younger participants and those of lower socioeconomic status (Blumberg & Luke, 2009). Some research suggests that telephone interviewing may also provide higher levels of disclosure on sensitive topics such as sexual abuse (DiNitto, et al., 2008). Furthermore, we chose this methodology as it provided the most efficient and cost-effective way to obtain a national sample, which allowed us to overcome a significant limitation in the current research on interpersonal violence among Latino women.

An adult respondent at each number was asked questions about the composition of the household (i.e., whether the number belonged to a residential household). Non-residential contacts were screened out (e.g., business, churches, college dormitories). If a residential household was reached, then the interviewer asked about the total number of age-eligible Latino females in the household. If there was only one eligible individual, that individual was asked to participate, if there was more than one eligible participant, then the "most recent/next birthday" method was used to decide which individual to interview. In this method, interviewers asked the Latino women residents whose birthday was the most recent or the next closest to the date of the phone interview. This is a widely used procedure because it permits unbiased systematic selection of respondents without needing full household enumeration (Salmon & Nichols, 1983). Participants were asked whether they preferred to conduct the interview in English or Spanish. If the interviewer was bilingual they would interview the participant in their preferred language, if the interviewer was only English speaking and the participant chose Spanish, the participant was called back by one of the bilingual interviewers.

Once a respondent was selected, they were read the informed consent and asked if they were willing to participate in the study. If they agreed to participate, they were interviewed at the current time or asked if they wished to be called back at a more convenient time. Before starting the survey questions, participants were given a code phrase to say ("OK, you're welcome") if they needed to suddenly end the call (e.g., due to safety or confidentiality concerns). Participants were then asked the various study instruments in the following order questions about state of social issues, demographic information, acculturation, lifetime victimization, help-seeking behaviors for the event that took place in the United States that was most upsetting, religiosity, gender role ideology, psychological symptoms, and posttraumatic symptoms. Some of the instruments were only asked of participants that reported a direct victimization experience; these were the HSQ (help-seeking), BMMSR (religiosity), BSRI – Short Form (gender role), and PCL (PTSD symptoms). All instruments had been translated into Spanish for the study with the exception of the TSI, PCL, and Brief ARSMA – II that already had established versions in Spanish. For participants with no victimization, the survey consisted

of a total of 89 questions. If a participant reported having a victimization incident, there were an

additional 24 follow-up questions per incident. For each witnessed victimization endorsed, there

were an additional three follow-up questions. For those who reported interpersonal

victimization, they were asked four additional instruments potentially resulting in 95 additional

items (the actual total number of additional questions depended on the participant's answers and

resultant skip patterns). The average time to complete the survey for all participants was 28

minutes.

Upon completing the survey, participants were asked if they felt distressed and were

offered a support hotline or callback to follow up with them. If the participant requested a

callback or the interviewer felt they should be follow-up with, the case was screened for follow

up. The study's principal investigator who is a bilingual licensed clinical psychologist called the

follow-up cases. He was tasked with making follow-up calls due to his extensive experience in

treating victims of abuse and trauma. On follow-up calls, the principal investigator asked for the

participant, once they responded he identified himself as someone who was calling to follow-up

on the study they had recently completed and asked them if this was a good time to talk prior to

querying about any concerns or distress associated with the study. During the call it was ensured

that the individual was no longer distressed and were provided with additional support

information if needed (e.g., local social service agencies, etc.). Approximately 1% of the sample

required follow-up. After completing the survey, participants were paid $10 for their

participation. The remuneration was sent along with a note that stated, "Thank you for

participating in our survey. If you have any questions about the project you can reach us at 1-

800-659-5432", giving no indication of the nature of the survey to protect participant safety and confidentiality.

An experienced survey research firm with specialization in doing surveys that ask about sensitive subjects (e.g., interpersonal violence) conducted the interviews using a Computer Assisted Telephone Interview (CATI) system. The interviewers were specifically trained on the SALAS survey and closely supervised during the data collection process. Only female interviewers were used since previous surveys using this methodology (e.g., National Violence Against Women [NVAW], Tjaden & Thoennes, 2000) showed that potential respondents were more likely to participate in the study if the interviewer is a woman. An initial attempt and four callbacks were made to reach a specific household, and then an additional three calls were made once a case was reached until final disposition is obtained (e.g., a completed survey or refusal). The Institutional Review Board (IRB) of Northeastern University authorized all study procedures with subsequent analyses also being approved by the IRB of The Pennsylvania State University.

III. RESULTS

Goal 1: Determine extent of sexual victimization in a sample of adult Latino females.

In calculating victimization rates, both unweighted and weighted figures are used. The weighted estimates use post-stratification weights that accounted for number of eligible respondents in the household, age cohorts, and household income. Detailed calculation procedures for sample weighing are provided in the SRBI Methods Report in the Appendix. The rate of sexual victimization for the sample was 17.2% (22.2% weighted). When broken down by the specific LTVH questions, 8.8% of the sample experienced a completed sexual assault, 8.9% experienced attempted sexual assault, and 11.4% experienced fondling or forced touch. Based on these different experiences, 48% of sexual assault victims reported more than one type of sexual victimization. When we broke down the results by adulthood and childhood sexual victimization, 7.6% of the sample experienced at least one adulthood sexual assault while 12.2% of the sample experienced at least one childhood sexual assault. Perpetrator rates show that adult sexual violence was most often perpetrated by either a spouse or partner (44.1% of adult sexual victimization) or someone else known to the victim (48.7% of adult sexual victimization). In childhood, the most common perpetrators were another relative (42.6%) or a non-family individual known to the victim (38.1%). In both adulthood and childhood sexual victimization, a minority of women were victimized by a stranger (30.3% and 15.21% respectively). Table 5 presents detailed results of victimization rates.

Table 5

Sexual Assault Victimization Rates

Victimization Type and Screener	n	Unweighted Rate [95% CI]	Weighted Rate [95% CI]	
Any Sexual Assault	344	17.2 [15.5, 18.8]	22.2 [19.1, 25.3]	
Sexual Assault	176	8.8 [7.6, 10.1]	11.2 [8.9, 13.4]	
Attempted Sexual Assault	178	8.9 [7.7, 10.2]	12.3 [9.8, 14.8]	
Fondling/Forced Touch	228	11.4 [10.1, 12.9]	15.1 [12.3, 17.8]	
Age/Perpetrator Breakdown				Unweighted % within Age Category
Any Adult Sexual Assault	152	7.6 [6.4, 8.8]	8.6 [6.7, 10.5]	
Parent	20	1.0 [0.6, 1.4]	1.1 [0.4, 1.8]	13.2
Other Relative	28	1.4	1.5	18.4

55

		[0.9, 1.9]	[0.7, 2.3]	
Partner/Spouse/Dating Rel.	67	3.4 [2.6, 4.1]	4.2 [2.8, 5.7]	44.1
Sibling	21	1.1 [0.6, 1.5]	1.1 [0.4, 1.8]	13.8
Other Known	74	3.7 [2.9, 4.5]	4.3 [3.0, 5.6]	48.7
Stranger	46	2.3 [1.6, 3.0]	2.0 [1.2, 2.8]	30.3
Multiple	20	1.0 [0.6, 1.4]	1.1 [0.4, 1.8]	13.2
Any Childhood Sexual Assault	244	12.2 [10.8, 13.6]	17.0 [14.1, 19.9]	
Parent	27	1.4 [0.8, 1.8]	2.3 [0.9, 3.7]	11.1
Other Relative	104	5.2 [4.2, 6.2]	7.2 [5.4, 9.1]	42.6
Partner/Spouse/Dating Rel.	24	1.2 [0.7, 1.7]	2.3 [0.9, 3.7]	9.8
Sibling	18	0.9 [0.5, 1.3]	1.2 [0.1, 2.3]	7.4
Other Known	93	4.7 [3.7, 5.6]	7.1 [4.7, 9.5]	38.1
Stranger	37	1.8 [1.3, 2.4]	2.0 [0.8, 3.2]	15.2
Multiple	8	0.4 [0.1, 0.6]	0.7 [0.0, 1.7]	3.3

Perpetrator categories were combined from the participant responses. Given how the data was collected, allowing participants to free respond on the perpetrator which was then categorized, a more detailed breakdown of perpetrator categories could be used in future data analyses. In addition, since country of origin and immigration data was collected, rates could be broken down by whether someone was an immigrant to the U.S., and within different groups of Latinos based on country of origin or ethnic background.

Goal 2: Determine the coexistence of other forms of victimization among those sexually victimized and the risk for subsequent victimization.

In total, 87.5% of the women who were sexually victimized also experienced at least one other form of victimization (e.g., sexual assault and physical assault) in their lifetime. The most frequent overlapping form of victimization was physical violence (60.2%) while the least frequent was witnessed victimization (45.1%). Table 6 presents detailed results on the overlap across the various forms of victimization.

Table 6

Co-morbid Lifetime Victimization Percentages for Sexually Victimized Participants

	Victimization Type				
	Any Other Victimization [95% CI]	Physical [95% CI]	Stalking [95% CI]	Threat [95% CI]	Witness [95% CI]
Sexual Assault	87.5 [85.0, 91.0]	60.2 [55.0, 65.4]	52.2 [46.9, 57.5]	57.6 [52.3, 62.8]	45.1 [39.8, 50.3]

When examining the breakdown based on childhood and adulthood events, Latino women who were sexually victimized in childhood also experienced high rates of other forms of childhood violence, with physical victimization being the most common (47.3%) co-existing victimization type. In adulthood, the most frequently co-occurring form of victimization for sexually victimized women was threats (55.9%). Table 7 presents detailed results of co-existing victimization in childhood and co-existing victimization in adulthood.

Table 7

Polyvictimization Percentages for Sexually Victimized Participants

	Child Victimization			
	Physical	Stalking	Threat	Witness
Child Sexual	47.3	29.9	22.4	27.8
	Adult Victimization			
	Physical	Stalking	Threat	Witness
Adult Sexual	43.4	48.0	55.9	23.7

In evaluating revictimization risk, we calculated the odds ratio that a victim of childhood sexual victimization would experience an adulthood victimization event across all forms of victimizations. All of the logistic models control for age and socioeconomic status. Results show that sexual victimization in childhood is a risk factor for any form of adulthood victimization (OR = 4.59, 95% CI [3.42, 6.16], $p < .001$) as well as a risk factor for all of the different types of victimizations in adulthood with the greatest risk being for threat victimization (OR = 4.56, 95% CI [3.37, 6.16], $p < .001$) and the lowest risk being for witnessed victimization (OR = 2.30, 95% CI [1.60, 2.29], $p < .001$). Table 8 shows the odds ratios for a victim of childhood sexual assault to experience another form of victimization in adulthood.

Table 8

Logistic Regression Revictimization Odds Ratios for Childhood Sexual Victimization

	Any OR [95% CI]	Sexual OR [95% CI]	Physical OR [95% CI]	Stalking OR [95% CI]	Threat OR [95% CI]	Witness OR [95% CI]
Age	1.00 [0.99, 1.00]	1.00 [0.99, 1.01]	0.99 [0.99, 1.00]	0.99 [0.98, 1.00]	0.99 [0.99, 1.00]	1.00 [0.99, 1.01]
SES	1.36*** [1.23, 1.49]	1.27** [1.10, 1.48]	1.00 [0.88, 1.15]	1.37*** [1.21, 1.55]	1.27*** [1.14, 1.43]	1.23** [1.08, 1.40]
Child Sexual	4.59*** [3.42, 6.16]	4.31*** [2.95, 6.31]	4.21*** [3.05, 5.81]	3.08*** [2.21, 4.30]	4.56*** [3.37, 6.16]	2.30*** [1.60, 2.29]
Nag R^2	.12	.09	.07	.08	.11	.04
X^2	181.55***	74.02***	76.93***	85.56***	131.91***	36.56***

* $p < .05$, ** $p < .01$, *** $p < .001$

Table 9 presents the sample victimization rates for the other forms of victimization that we evaluated in addition to sexual violence among the full sample of 2,000 Latino women.

Table 9

Victimization Rates for Non-sexual Forms of Victimization

Any Victimization			
Physical	Stalking	Threat	Witness
22.2	18.3	21.1	20.1
Adult Victimization			
Physical	Stalking	Threat	Witness
13.0	12.0	16.4	10.8
Child Victimization			
Physical	Stalking	Threat	Witness
15.2	8.2	6.4	9.9

Overall, 43.5% of the sample reported at least one lifetime victimization experience, with 28.8% reporting at least one childhood event and 31.9% reporting at least one adulthood event. In examining the various forms of victimization, we found that 26.7% of women had more than one type of victimization in their lifetime (e.g., stalking and physical assault or physical assault and sexual assault), which means that 61.3% of victimized women experience two or more different forms of victimization.

Goal 3: Examine formal service utilization among sexually victimized Latino women.

The majority (66.5%) of women who experienced sexual victimization selected sexual victimization as the index incident for help-seeking questions, indicating it was the most distressful victimization experience. Analyses on help-seeking responses focus on these respondents. Formal help-seeking included seeking medical attention, respondent reporting the incident to police, going to a social service agency, obtaining a restraining order or filing

criminal charges. About 21% of the respondents sought one or more types of formal help. The

most common type of formal help-seeking was medical services among women who reported

injuries. The main injures reported, among those injured, include large bruises (45.9%), small

bruises (37.8%), injuries inside the body (27%), and sprains, broken bones, or broken teeth

(13.5%). Criminal justice responses were not commonly sought.

Table 10

Help-seeking Responses of Those who Reported Sexual Victimization as Most Distressful (n = 212)

Response	n	%
Injured	39	18.4
Doctor, medical center, hospital	16	41.0
Police[a]	14	6.6
Social service agency	21	9.9
Restraining order	15	7.1
Criminal charges	13	6.1
ANY FORMAL HELP-SEEKING	44	20.8

[a] This refers to sexual victims who reported the victimization to the police themselves as an examination of victims' help-seeking is central here. An additional 16 participants indicated that another person reported the index sexual victimization. The full 30 reports to the police are used for analyses below.

Specific details were gathered about the response of police and the court process and the

participant's satisfaction with these criminal justice resources. Calling the police, either by the

victim herself or someone else, resulted in an arrest of the assailant in almost 50% of the cases.

Restraining orders were uncommon among sexual victims and were violated by a third of the assailants. Criminal charges were the least likely formal help-seeking mode of sexual victims and 54% of filed criminal charges ($n = 7$) resulted in sentences among this sample. Within the broader context of those who reported sexual victimization as most distressful, only 3% resulted in sentencing of the assailant. In general, respondents were more satisfied than dissatisfied with both the police and courts and most satisfied with the courts.

Table 11

Detail of Police and Court Help-seeking Responses

	n	%
Police	30	14.2[a]
See you in person to take a report	14	46.7
Arrest him/her	14	46.7
Give you advice on how to protect yourself	8	26.7
Refer you to services	7	23.3
Nothing	5	16.7
Refer you to court	4	13.3
Take you somewhere	1	3.3
Court		
Restraining order	15	7.2[a]
Violate restraining order	5	33.3
Filed criminal charges	13	6.3[a]
Convicted	4	30.8
Pled guilty	4	30.8
Acquitted	1	7.7

Charges dropped	1	7.7
Other	3	23.1
	M	*SD*
Satisfaction with police response[b]	2.4	1.2
Satisfaction with treatment during court process[b]	3.0	1.1

[a] Percentages indicate of sexual victims. Remaining percentages are of subsets that enacted either police or court formal help-seeking
[b] Reported on a scale of 1 'very satisfied' to 5 'very dissatisfied'

Medical and social service help-seeking details were gathered along with a rating of helpfulness for each response. The predominant medical service sought was the emergency room (37.5% of injured women), but it received the lowest helpfulness rating of medical services. Similarly, the most common social service sought, non-specialized counseling/therapist, was also rated as least helpful in relation to the other social services. Specialized services like abuse counseling, shelter, domestic violence counseling and crisis line were rated as somewhat to very helpful, but were uncommonly sought. In fact, only 3.3% of sexual victims went to any of these four specialized services.

Table 12

Detail of Medical and Social Service Help-seeking Responses

Help-seeking response	n	%	Helfulness[a] (SD)
Medical service sought			
Visited emergency room	6	37.5	2.8 (2.0)
Visited a medical center	5	31.3	4.4 (1.3)
Visited my doctor	3	18.8	4.0 (1.7)
Was hospitalized	3	18.8	5.0 (0)
Referred or visited psychologist/psychiatrist	1	6.3	5.0 (0)
Social service agency sought			
Other counseling/ therapist	7	33.3	3 (1.9)
Abuse/trauma counseling	3	14.3	4.5 (.7)
Domestic violence counseling	3	14.3	4.7 (.6)
Mental health center	3	14.3	4.5 (.7)
Shelter	2	9.5	4 (0)
Crisis line	1	4.8	4 (0)

[a] Reported on a scale of 1 'very unhelpful' to 5 'very helpful'

To better understand women's responses, women who employed formal help-seeking were asked how each could improve. Those who did not seek a specific type of formal help-seeking were asked why they did not seek it. Respondents indicated that police could improve services by charging or arresting assailants and courts could improve by taking reports more seriously. Respondents also suggested offering more advice for medical and social service agencies. Here the respondents restated the importance of reporting their victimization. The

main reasons for not seeking formal help included fear, shame and being too young.

Table 13

Ways to Improve Services and Reasons why Services Not Sought

	To Improve	Why Not Sought
Police	(*n* = 30) Charge/ arrest/ lock-up person (23.3%) Be more supportive (13.3%) Take complaint more seriously (10%) Not sure (10%) Refer/take to services (6.7%)	(*n* = 131) Fear of offender (29.4%) Too young (17.2%) Didn't think of it (12.8%) Wouldn't be believed (9.4%) Shame (8.9%) Wanted to keep incident private (8.9%)
Courts	(*n* =5) Taken report more seriously (60%) Provide/suggest treatment (40%) Provide more legal help (20%)	(*n* = 193) Too young (18.7%) Fear of offender (16.1%) Didn't think of it (13%) Wanted to keep incident private (10.9%) Shame (9.3%)
Medical	(*n* = 7) Provide counseling/offer advice (42.9%) Reported it (42.9%) More/better treatment (28.6%) Financial help (28.6%) Been more supportive (28.6%)	(*n*= 23) Other (26.1%) Shame (17.4%) I didn't think of it (13%) Fear of further abuse (8.7%) Too young (8.7%)
Agency	(*n* = 2) Provide counseling/offer advice (50%) Reported it (50%)	(*n* = 189) Didn't think of it (26.5%) Didn't know of any (13.2%) Shame (9%) Wanted to keep incident private (9%) No agency available in area (7.9%)

For respondents who experienced only one sexual victimization, it was possible to link

specific sexual victimization types to help-seeking responses. A chi-square test of independence

revealed no relationship between type of sexual victimization and rate of formal help-seeking (X^2

$(2) = 2.99$, $p = .23$).

Table 14

Rate of Help-seeking by Sexual Victimization Type (*n* = 103)

	% that Sought Formal Help-seeking
Coerced sexual activity	15.8%
Attempted sexual coercion	20.0%
Fondling	7.4%

Formal help-seeking was examined in relation to psychosocial functioning, namely, post-traumatic symptoms, depression, anger/irritability, anxiety, and dissociation. A series of multiple regressions with demographic controls of age and socio-economic status revealed that formal help-seeking had no significant relationship with psychosocial functioning, contributing little to the variance. Reasons for this non-significant association may include that many help-seeking services did not target mental health specifically; recent psychological functioning was measured, not controlling for how long ago the victimization occurred nor the timing of the help-seeking; and the large number of non-victimization related variables that influence psychological functioning (e.g., economic stress). The count of victimizations did significantly influence post-traumatic symptoms ($B = 1.08$, $p = .04$) and depression ($B = .69$, $p = .04$) with increased victimization relating to increased post-traumatic symptoms and depression. Detailed results are presented in Tables 15 and 16.

Table 15

Formal Help-Seeking and Psychosocial Outcomes Among Women who Reported Sexual Victimization as Most Distressful (n = 211)

	PCL-Total B [95% CI]	Depression B [95% CI]	Anger B [95% CI]	Anxiety B [95% CI]	Dissociation B [95% CI]
Age	-0.17* [-0.33, -0.01]	0.01 [-0.10, 0.12]	-0.10 [-0.21, 0.02]	-0.03 [-0.15, 0.09]	-0.10 [-0.23, 0.04]
SES	-2.09* [-3.91, -0.28]	-1.05 [-2.29, -0.20]	-0.62 [-1.93, 0.69]	-1.15 [-2.48, 0.19]	-2.30** [-3.78, -0.80]
Vic count	1.08* [0.07, 2.08]	0.69* [-0.01, 1.38]	0.47 [-0.25, 1.20]	0.61 [-0.13, 1.36]	0.39 [-0.44, 1.22]
Any formal help	0.43 [-5.15, 6.02]	-0.97 [-4.79, 2.85]	-4.31 [-8.32, -0.29]	-2.49 [-6.58, 1.61]	-2.23 [-6.80, 2.34]
R^2	0.07	0.03	0.04	0.03	0.06
F	3.82**	1.60	1.94	1.53	3.05*

*p < .05 **p < .01

67

Table 16

Formal Help-Seeking Types and Psychosocial Outcomes Among Women Reporting Sexual Victimization as Most Distressful (n = 209)

	PCL-Total B	[95% CI]	Depression B	[95% CI]	Anger B	[95% CI]	Anxiety B	[95% CI]	Dissociation B	[95% CI]
Age	-0.18*	[-0.35, -0.02]	0.02	[-0.10, 0.13]	-0.09	[-0.21, 0.29]	-0.03	[-0.15, 0.09]	-0.11	[-0.24, 0.03]
SES	-2.15*	[-3.99, -0.31]	-1.15	[-2.41, 0.10]	-0.66	[-1.99, -0.68]	-1.26	[-2.61, 0.08]	-2.31**	[-3.81, -0.82]
Vic count	1.08*	[0.06, 2.11]	0.73*	[0.03, 1.43]	0.41	[-0.33, 1.15]	0.64	[-0.11, 1.38]	0.39	[-0.44, 1.22]
Police	-0.95	[-11.06, 9.17]	-4.73	[-11.63, 2.17]	-4.13	[-11.44, 3.19]	-3.20	[-10.58, 4.18]	-2.89	[-11.11, 5.34]
Rest Order	-1.10	[-10.31, 8.11]	0.08	[-6.21, 6.36]	-1.55	[-8.21, 5.12]	1.02	[-5.71, 7.75]	3.53	[-3.96, 11.03]
Criminal Charges	2.09	[-8.36, 12.54]	-2.05	[-9.18, 5.08]	-0.48	[-8.04, 7.08]	-4.52	[-12.16, 3.11]	-1.05	[-9.55, 7.45]
Social Service	-0.92	[-9.17, 7.33]	0.78	[-4.85, 6.41]	-1.43	[-7.40, -4.54]	0.17	[-5.85, 6.20]	-4.29	[-11.00, 2.42]
R^2	0.07		0.04		0.03		0.04		0.07	
F	2.23*		1.30		0.93		1.15		2.18*	

*$p < .05$ **$p < .01$

68

Goal 4: Examine informal help-seeking among sexually victimized Latino women.

Informal help-seeking, as measured by talking to someone about the sexual victimization incident, was more common than formal help-seeking. Almost 60% of sexual victims talked to someone about the incident. Disclosure to friends was most common at 31.7%, but disclosure to family was also quite common, with 30.9% disclosing to parents. The most helpful confidants according to respondents were other family members and the least helpful were parents, as reported in Table 17.

Table 17

Informal Help-seeking Sourced and Rated Helpfulness

Disclosure	N	%	Helpfulness Mean (SD)[a]
Talk to someone else	123	58.3	
Confidant			
Friend, neighbor	39	31.7	4.3 (.8)
Parents	38	30.9	3.7 (1.5)
Siblings	22	17.9	3.8 (1.3)
Husband/partner	17	13.8	4.7 (.6)
Minister/ clergy	16	13.0	3.8 (1.5)
Other family	10	8.1	4.8 (.5)

[a] Reported on a scale of 1 'very unhelpful' to 5 'very helpful'

Confidants could improve by being more supportive and reporting the incident, according to respondents. This theme is similar to the recommendations for formal help-seeking. Women who did not disclose the incident reported shame as the main reason for keeping the incident to themselves (see Table 18 below).

Table 18

Ways to Improve Disclosure Events and Reasons why Disclosure not Sought

	To Improve	Why Not Sought
Informal	($n = 26$)	($n = 88$)
	Been more supportive (42.3%)	Shame (31.8%)
	Reported it (19.2%)	Didn't think of it (19.3%)
	A/O mentions (15.4%)	Fear of further abuse (13.6%)
	Provide counseling/advice (11.5%)	Wanted to keep incident private
	Confront person involved (11.5%)	(12.5%)
		Wouldn't be believed (9.1%)
		Didn't want/need help (9.1%)

For respondents who experienced only one sexual victimization, it was possible to link specific sexual victimization types to help-seeking responses. A chi-square test of independence revealed no relationship between type of sexual victimization and rate of informal help-seeking (X^2 (2) = 1.89, p = .39).

Table 19

Rate of Help-seeking by Sexual Victimization Type (n = 102)

	% that Sought Informal Help-seeking
Coerced sexual activity	42.1%
Attempted sexual coercion	62.1%
Fondling	51.9%

Informal help-seeking was examined in relation to psychosocial functioning, namely, post-traumatic symptoms, depression, anger/irritability, anxiety, and dissociation. A series of multiple regressions with demographic controls of age and socio-economic status revealed that informal help-seeking was related to one measure of psychosocial functioning. Talking to someone about the sexual victimization was significantly predictive of decreased depression (*B* =

-3.58, $p = .02$). Detailed results are available in Table 20. As with formal help-seeking, it appears that psychological functioning is influenced by factors other than informal-seeking per se—perhaps concurrent non-victimization stressors, quality of help received, and response of social network.

Table 20

Informal Help-Seeking and Psychosocial Outcomes Among Women who Reported Sexual Victimization as Most Distressful (n = 210)

	PCL-Total		Depression		Anger		Anxiety		Dissociation	
	B	[95% CI]	B	[95% CI]	B	[95% CI]	B	[95% CI]	B	[95% CI]
Age	-0.18*	[-0.34, -0.02]	0.01	[-0.10, 0.11]	-0.09	[-0.21, 0.03]	-0.03	[-0.15, 0.09]	-0.10	[-0.23, 0.04]
SES	-1.93*	[-3.80, -0.07]	-0.74	[-2.01, 0.52]	-0.45	[-1.80, 0.91]	-0.99	[-2.37, 0.38]	-2.15**	[-3.68, -0.61]
Vic count	1.11*	[0.14, 2.09]	0.67*	[0.01, 1.34]	0.29	[-0.42, 1.00]	0.51	[-0.21, 1.23]	0.30	[-0.50, 1.10]
Any informal help	-1.81	[-6.31, 2.70]	-3.58*	[-6.63, -0.54]	-1.85	[-5.12, 1.42]	-1.52	[-4.83, 1.80]	-1.57	[-5.26, 2.13]
R^2	0.07		0.05		0.02		0.02		0.05	
F	3.70**		2.76*		1.10		1.28		2.81*	

*$p < .05$ **$p < .01$

Table 21

Specific Types of Informal Help-Seeking and Psychosocial Outcomes Among Women who Reported Sexual Victimization as Most Distressful (n= 210)

	PCL-Total B [95% CI]	Depression B [95% CI]	Anger B [95% CI]	Anxiety B [95% CI]	Dissociation B [95% CI]
Age	-0.21* [-0.37, -0.04]	0.02 [-0.10, 0.13]	-0.08 [-0.21, 0.04]	-0.03 [-0.15, 0.10]	-0.11 [-0.25, 0.03]
SES	-1.97* [-3.88, -0.06]	-0.71 [-2.00, 0.58]	-0.58 [-1.97, 0.81]	-1.12 [-2.52, 0.28]	-2.11** [-3.66, -0.55]
Vic count	1.12* [0.11, 2.13]	0.67* [-0.01, 1.36]	0.30 [-0.43, 1.03]	0.55 [-0.19, 1.30]	0.31 [-0.51, 1.13]
Parents	-3.65 [-9.54, 2.24]	-4.21* [-8.20, -0.22]	-1.95 [-6.23, 2.34]	-2.13 [-6.45, 2.18]	-4.21 [-9.00, 0.59]
Sibling	0.78 [-6.56, 8.10]	-1.61 [-6.58, 3.35]	-0.37 [-5.70, 4.96]	-0.75 [-6.12, 4.62]	1.21 [-4.76, 7.19]
Other family	-0.10 [-9.70, 9.50]	-0.08 [-6.58, 6.42]	-3.67 [-10.65, 3.31]	-1.82 [-8.85, 5.21]	-1.38 [-9.20, 6.44]
Husband/Partner	2.72 [-5.47, 10.91]	-0.43 [-5.98, 5.11]	2.65 [-3.30, 8.61]	2.34 [-3.66, 8.33]	4.14 [-2.53, 10.81]
Friend/ neighbor	-2.23 [-8.14, 3.67]	-0.15 [-4.15, 3.85]	0.70 [-3.60, 4.98]	0.94 [-3.39, 5.26]	-1.41 [-6.25, 3.40]

Professional	4.24 [-8.27, 16.76]	-4.55 [-13.03, 3.92]	-0.50 [-9.60, 8.60]	1.36 [-7.81, 10.53]	-1.23 [-11.42, 8.98]
Clergy	-2.81 [-11.18, 5.56]	-3.69 [-9.36, 1.98]	-0.77 [-6.85, 5.32]	-4.97 [-11.10, 1.16]	-1.85 [-8.66, 4.97]
R^2	0.08	0.06	0.03	0.05	0.08
F	1.77	1.36	0.67	1.00	1.69

*$p < .05$ **$p < .01$

Goal 5: Examine culturally-relevant factors associated with experience and responses to sexual violence.

The first analysis examines the likelihood of reporting any sexual victimization by age, socio-economic status, immigrant status, and Anglo orientation. An increase in age is associated with a decrease in odds of reporting sexual victimization (OR = .98, $p < .001$). Higher SES was associated with an increase in odds of sexual victimization (OR = 1.23, $p < .001$). Being an immigrant was significantly predictive of decreased odds of sexual victimization (OR = .60, $p < .001$). Anglo acculturation was associated with increased odds of sexual victimization. Together these findings show the importance of a culturally-based understanding of sexual victimization.

Table 22

Variables Predicting Sexual Victimization (n = 1866)

Predictor	OR	p	95 % CI
Age	.98	.00	[0.98, 0.99]
SES	1.23	.00	[1.09, 1.39]
Immigrant status	.60	.00	[0.45, 0.80]
Anglo orientation	1.06	.00	[1.03, 1.08]
Nag R^2	.12		
X^2	136.89	.00	

The next analysis focused on the relationship between cultural factors and the number of sexual victimizations. In Table 23, we see that increased Anglo orientation is significantly predictive of an increased number of sexual victimizations ($B = .02, p = .03$).

Table 23

Cultural Factors and the Extent of Sexual Victimization (n = 285)

Predictor	B	p	95 % CI
Age	-0.00	0.42	[-0.01, 0.00]
SES	0.03	0.45	[-0.05, 0.12]
Immigrant status	-0.05	0.63	[-0.26, 0.16]
Anglo orientation	0.02	0.03	[0.00, 0.04]
Masculine	0.01	0.36	[-0.01, 0.02]
Feminine	-0.01	0.52	[-0.02, 0.01]
Positive Religious Coping	-0.01	0.83	[-0.05, 0.04]
Negative Religious Coping	0.02	0.58	[-0.04, 0.08]
R^2	0.05		
F	1.84	0.07	

Next, the influence of cultural factors on psychosocial outcomes among sexual victims was explored in a series of multiple regressions (see Table 24). Masculine gender role was significantly associated with post-traumatic stress ($B = .28$, $p = .03$) anger/irritability ($B = .38$, $p < .001$) and anxiety ($B = .19$, $p = .05$). Religious coping influenced psychosocial outcomes with positive religious coping significantly predicting decreased depression ($B = -.60$, $p = .03$) and negative religious coping predicting increased post-traumatic stress ($B = 1.73$, $p < .01$), depression ($B = 1.12$, $p < .01$) and anxiety ($B = .82$, $p = .05$).

76

Table 24

Cultural Factors and Psychosocial Outcomes Among Sexually Victimized Women (n = 285)

	PCL-Total B [95% CI]	Depression B [95% CI]	Anger B [95% CI]	Anxiety B [95% CI]	Dissociation B [95% CI]
Age	-0.06 [-0.19, 0.08]	0.10* [0.00, 0.19]	-0.01 [-0.11, 0.09]	0.07 [-0.03, 0.17]	0.00 [-0.12, 0.12]
SES	-2.18** [-3.75, -0.61]	-1.18* [-2.26, -0.11]	-0.94 [-2.04, 0.16]	-1.00 [-2.18, 0.17]	-1.98** [-3.29, -0.67]
Vic count	1.12** [0.35, 1.90]	0.64* [0.11, 1.17]	0.26 [-0.28, 0.80]	0.50 [-0.08, 1.08]	0.47 [-0.18, 1.12]
Immigrant	2.50 [-1.37, 6.38]	2.12 [-0.53, 4.77]	-1.15 [-3.87, 1.57]	2.45 [-0.46, 5.36]	2.30 [-0.93, 5.54]
Anglo Orientation	-0.12 [-0.50, 0.25]	-0.05 [-0.31, 0.20]	-0.01 [-0.28, 0.25]	-0.12 [-0.40, 0.16]	-0.10 [-0.41, 0.21]
Masculine	0.28* [0.02, 0.53]	0.06 [-0.11, 0.24]	0.38*** [0.20, 0.56]	0.19* [-0.00, 0.38]	0.21 [-0.00, 0.42]
Feminine	-0.17 [-0.46, 0.12]	0.07 [-0.13, 0.27]	-0.12 [-0.32, 0.10]	-0.05 [-0.27, 0.17]	0.04 [-0.21, 0.28]
Pos Religious Coping	-0.26 [-1.07, 0.55]	-0.60* [-1.16, -0.05]	-0.81 [-1.38, -0.25]	-0.72 [-1.33, -0.11]	-0.32 [-0.99, 0.36]
Neg Religious	1.73**	1.12**	1.46	0.82*	1.48

Coping	[0.65, 2.81]	[0.38, 1.86]	[0.70, 2.21]	[0.10, 1.63]	[0.58, 2.39]
R^2	0.16	0.14	0.21	0.12	0.14
F	5.88***	5.15***	7.86***	4.24***	5.15***

*$p < .05$ **$p < .01$ ***$p < .001$

Cultural factors were also tested in relation to help-seeking responses among those who reported sexual victimization as the most distressful. Anglo orientation was related to an increase in odds of formal help-seeking in general (OR = 1.10, p = .04), and getting social services in particular (OR = 1.15, p = .05). See Table 25.

With relation to informal help-seeking, none of the cultural factors significantly altered the odds of informal help-seeking in general or any particular confidant. Detailed results are shown in Table 26.

Table 25

Logistic Regression of Cultural Factors Predicting Formal Help-Seeking Among Those who Reported Sexual Victimization as Most

Distressful

	Dependent Variable (Formal Help-Seeking)					
Predictor	Any formal OR [95% CI]	Police OR [95% CI]	Restraining Order OR [95% CI]	Criminal Charges OR [95% CI]	Social Services OR [95% CI]	Medical OR [95%CI]
Age	0.98 [0.95, 1.01]	1.00 [0.95, 1.04]	1.00 [0.94, 1.04]	0.95 [1.00, 1.01]	0.96 [0.91, 1.00]	1.09 [0.98, 1.21]
SES	0.82 [0.57, 1.18]	0.66 [0.36, 1.21]	0.79 [0.44, 1.41]	0.56 [0.27, 1.15]	1.06 [0.65, 1.70]	1.51 [0.50, 4.50]
Vic count	1.36*** [1.15, 1.60]	1.18 [0.94, 1.49]	1.29* [1.01, 1.63]	1.59*** [1.20, 2.12]	1.42** [1.13, 1.78]	1.62* [1.08, 2.44]
Immigrant	1.64 [0.68, 3.97]	0.42 [0.09, 1.89]	0.97 [0.24, 3.97]	1.73 [0.34, 8.72]	1.72 [0.52, 5.70]	3.44 [0.28, 42.16]
Anglo	1.10* [1.01, 1.20]	1.00 [0.88, 1.13]	1.02 [0.89, 1.16]	1.14 [0.98, 1.33]	1.15* [1.00, 1.31]	1.09 [0.88, 1.34]
Masculine	1.00 [0.95, 1.07]	1.10 [1.00, 1.22]	1.01 [0.92, 1.11]	1.11 [0.98, 1.26]	1.00 [0.92, 1.10]	1.07 [0.90, 1.27]
Feminine	1.04 [0.96, 1.12]	1.02 [0.91, 1.14]	1.05 [0.92, 1.19]	1.09 [0.93, 1.29]	1.09 [0.96, 1.22]	1.03 [0.81, 1.31]

Pos Religious Coping	0.97 [0.81, 1.16]	1.07 [0.81, 1.42]	0.96 [0.70, 1.32]	1.19 [0.85, 1.67]	0.92 [0.73, 1.17]	0.88 [0.49, 1.58]
Neg Religious Coping	1.00 [0.78, 1.28]	0.95 [0.65, 1.38]	0.41 [0.18, 0.93]	1.04 [0.69, 1.57]	1.11 [0.79, 1.57]	0.90 [0.45, 1.79]
Nag R^2	0.18	0.13	0.19	0.33	0.24	0.38
X^2	22.73**	10.05	15.14	24.47**	21.71**	11.07
N	180	180	180	180	179	33

$p < .05$, ** $p < .01$, *** $p < .001$

Table 26

Logistic Regression of Cultural Factors Predicting Informal Help-Seeking Among Those who Reported Sexual Victimization as Most

Distressful (n = 179)

| | | | | | Dependent Variable (Informal Help-Seeking) | | | | |
| | | | | | Other | | | | |
Predictor	Any Informal OR [95% CI]	Parents OR [95% CI]	Sibling CR [95% CI]	Family OR [95% CI]	Partner OR [95% CI]	Friend OR [95% CI]	Clergy OR [95% CI]	Prof OR [95% CI]
Age	0.99 [0.97, 1.02]	0.98 [0.95, 1.02]	1.10 [0.98, 1.06]	1.00 [0.95, 1.05]	1.01 [0.97, 1.07]	0.97 [0.94, 1.00]	0.99 [0.95, 1.03]	1.09* [1.00, 1.18]
SES	1.09 [0.82, 1.47]	1.31 [0.93, 1.85]	0.82 [0.50, 1.34]	0.56 [0.29, 1.09]	1.05 [0.61, 1.80]	1.07 [0.75, 1.52]	0.98 [0.58, 1.67]	1.80 [0.80, 4.06]
Vic count	1.06 [0.92, 1.23]	0.92 [0.76, 1.11]	1.29** [1.06, 1.57]	0.94 [0.70, 1.26]	0.86 [0.64, 1.14]	1.05 [0.89, 1.25]	1.09 [0.86, 1.38]	1.14 [0.77, 1.70]
Immigrant	0.62 [0.30, 1.24]	0.83 [0.34, 2.02]	0.74 [0.23, 2.38]	0.79 [0.18, 3.43]	0.37 [0.09, 1.52]	1.22 [0.51, 2.93]	0.53 [0.13, 2.12]	0.13 [0.10, 1.66]
Anglo	1.03 [0.97, 1.10]	1.10 [1.00, 1.22]	0.96 [0.87, 1.07]	1.17 [1.00, 1.38]	1.00 [0.88, 1.14]	1.03 [0.95, 1.12]	0.96 [0.85, 1.09]	0.90 [0.70, 1.14]
Masculine	1.00 [0.96, 1.05]	1.04 [0.97, 1.11]	0.95 [0.89, 1.02]	1.06 [0.96, 1.18]	0.94 [0.87, 1.01]	0.99 [0.93, 1.04]	1.07 [0.98, 1.18]	1.11 [0.94, 1.32]
Feminine	0.99 [0.93, 1.05]	1.04 [0.96, 1.12]	0.98 [0.90, 1.07]	0.97 [0.86, 1.08]	1.04 [0.92, 1.17]	0.97 [0.91, 1.04]	1.01 [0.91, 1.13]	0.98 [0.83, 1.15]

82

Pos Religious Cop	1.08 [0.93, 1.25]	0.98 [0.82, 1.17]	1.09 [0.85, 1.39]	1.10 [0.81, 1.47]	1.18 [0.85, 1.63]	0.92 [0.77, 1.09]	1.14 [0.87, 1.50]	0.93 [0.61, 1.41]
Neg Religious Cop	1.08 [0.88, 1.32]	1.24 [0.96, 1.59]	0.98 [0.72, 1.34]	1.02 [0.69, 1.51]	0.89 [0.57, 1.40]	0.95 [0.73, 1.23]	1.25 [0.91, 1.71]	1.14 [0.57, 2.28]
Nag R^2	0.07	0.15	0.11	0.12	0.14	0.09	0.08	0.26
X^2	9.84	17.62*	10.63	8.22	10.36	10.29	6.32	12.10

* $p < .05$, ** $p < .01$

83

Goal 6: Determine the psychosocial impact of sexual victimization on Latino women.

In evaluating the psychosocial impact of victimization we examined the incremental contribution of having only experienced childhood sexual abuse, only experienced sexual assault in adulthood, or the contribution of the total number of reported sexual assault incidents (regardless of when it occurred) while controlling for age and socioeconomic status. The psychosocial variables that were evaluated included Depression ($M = 49.18$, $SD = 9.50$), Anxiety ($M = 50.64$, $SD = 11.42$), Anger ($M = 48.29$, $SD = 10.13$), and Dissociation ($M = 50.64$, $SD = 11.86$), as measured by the TSI and posttraumatic symptomatology as measured by PCL ($M = 32.76$, $SD = 15.09$). All models use the full sample ($N = 2,000$) except for the correlations/models evaluating PTSD which only use the subsample of personally victimized individuals ($N = 732$) due to the PCL being administered only to the women who had been directly victimized (i.e., not including witnessed victimization).

The second set of regressions evaluated the incremental contribution of sexual assault incidents and count of total victimization experiences to determine whether sexual victimization incrementally predicts psychological distress while accounting for overall victimization while controlling for age and socioeconomic status. Bivariate correlations for all the variables used in the regression models are presented in Table 27.

The regression analysis examining the role of child only, adult only, and total number of sexual assault experiences found that the total number of sexual assault incidents was the best predictor of depression, anxiety, and PTSD symptomatology, while child only, adult only, and the total number of sexual assault incidents all significantly predicted dissociation and anger symptoms. In examining the role of the total number of victimization experiences, this was the best predictor across all forms of psychological symptoms above and beyond the impact of

sexual assault incidents. Detailed regression results are presented in Tables 28 and 29.

Table 27

Bivariate Correlations of Sexual Assault and Total Victimization Regression Variables

Variable	1	2	3	4	5	6	7	8	9	10	11
1. Age	---										
2. SES	-.11***	---									
3. Child Only	-.14***	.13***	---								
4. Adult Only	-.02	.05*	-.07**	---							
5. Total Sexual Assaults	-.12***	.20***	.57***	.37***	---						
6. Vict. Count	-.16***	.18***	.45***	.35***	.76***	---					
7. Depression	.09***	-.11***	.08***	.10***	.15***	.21***	---				
8. Anxiety	.07**	-.07**	.05*	.08***	.11***	.17***	.76***	---			
9. Anger	-.05*	.02	.14***	.12***	.20***	.25***	.68***	.69***	---		
10. Dissociation	-.02	-.08***	.10***	.12***	.15***	.22***	.75***	.74***	.72***	---	
11. PTSD[a]	-.07	-.12**	.08*	.11**	.19***	.28***	.68***	.68***	.61***	.65***	---

[a] Only asked of victimized subsample, n = 732, *p < .05, **p < .01, ***p < .001

86

Table 28

Linear Regressions of Childhood Sexual Victimization and Psychological Distress

	PCL-Total B [95% CI]	Depression B [95% CI]	Anger B [95% CI]	Anxiety B [95% CI]	Dissociation B [95% CI]
Age	-0.06 [-0.14, 0.01]	0.06*** [0.03, 0.08]	-0.02 [-0.05, 0.01]	0.05*** [0.02, 0.83]	-0.01 [-0.04, 0.03]
SES	-2.03*** [-2.98, -1.08]	-1.33*** [-1.75, -0.91]	-0.22 [-0.67, 0.23]	-1.03*** [-1.54, -0.52]	-1.34*** [-1.86, -0.81]
Child Sexual Only	0.57 [-2.41, 3.55]	1.16 [-0.66, 2.97]	2.37* [0.42, 4.32]	0.46 [-1.76, 2.68]	2.58* [0.29, 4.86]
Adult Sexual Only	3.05 [-0.53, 6.63]	2.55* [0.36, 4.74]	3.69** [1.34, 6.04]	2.44 [-0.24, 5.12]	4.86*** [2.10, 7.61]
Total Sexual Assaults	2.45*** [1.28, 3.62]	1.73*** [1.02, 2.45]	1.61*** [0.84, 2.38]	1.54*** [0.66, 2.41]	1.52*** [0.62, 2.42]
R^2	.07	.06	.05	.03	.04
F	10.31***	22.83***	18.56***	10.97***	17.00***

* $p < .05$, ** $p < .01$, *** $p < .001$

Table 29

Linear Regressions of Childhood Sexual Victimization, Total Victimization, and Psychological Distress

	PCL-Total B [95% CI]	Depression B [95% CI]	Anger B [95% CI]	Anxiety B [95% CI]	Dissociation B [95% CI]
Age	-0.04 [-0.12, 0.03]	0.07*** [0.04, 0.09]	-0.01 [-0.04, 0.02]	0.06*** [0.03, 0.09]	0.01 [-0.03, 0.04]
SES	-1.90*** [-2.83, -0.97]	-1.39*** [-1.79, -0.97]	-0.28 [-0.72, 0.17]	-1.09*** [-1.59, -0.58]	-1.41*** [-1.93, -0.89]
Total Sexual Assaults	0.58 [-0.66, 1.84]	0.04 [-0.74, 0.81]	0.11 [-0.72, 0.95]	-0.58 [-1.53, 0.36]	-0.48 [-1.45, 0.49]
Victimization Count	1.82*** [1.14, 2.50]	1.24*** [0.91, 1.56]	1.33*** [0.98, 1.68]	1.39*** [0.99, 1.79]	1.70*** [1.29, 2.11]
R^2	.10	.08	.07	.05	.07
F	19.51***	41.65***	34.54***	24.81***	34.93***

* $p < .05$, ** $p < .01$, *** $p < .001$

IV. CONCLUSIONS

The Sexual Assault Among Latinas (SALAS) Study adds to the literature by using a national sample to gather estimates of sexual, physical, stalking, threatened, and witnessed violence for Latino women. The first two goals of the study focused on determining the extent of sexual victimization alone (Goal 1) and the overlap of sexual victimization with other forms of victimization (Goal 2). Furthermore, the study also queried responses to victimization, forming the bases of Goals 3 and 4 that examined the rates and correlates of formal and informal help-seeking, respectively. Another distinguishing component of SALAS is the investigation of the role of culturally - relevant variables such as religiosity, gender role ideology and acculturation on responses to victimization. Goal 5 examined each of these in relation to rates of victimization, psychosocial outcomes and help-seeking. The psychosocial impact of sexual victimization was highlighted in Goal 6 by examining trauma symptoms and PTSD.

The SALAS sample, garnered from high-density Latino areas, was heavily Mexican-American (72% of the full sample either Mexican born or of Mexican ancestry) and Cuban (14% of the full sample either Cuban born or of Cuban ancestry). As of the 2000 Census, 58.5% of Latinos identified as Mexican and 3.5% as Cuban (Guzman, 2001). Thus, these groups may be more likely to live in high density Latino areas compared to other Latino groups. Other variations from the national Latino population as reported by the Census Bureau, includes an elevated median age, a higher level of education, and smaller proportion of being born in the U.S. or being U.S. citizens compared to Census figures (Guzman, 2001; Ramirez, 2004; U.S. Census Bureau, 2000). These differences, some of which were accounted for by post-stratification weights and applied to rates figures presented, should be kept in mind while generalizing to the Latino population as a whole. A further caveat, participants self-identified as

Latino and while they reported birthplace or ancestry congruent with this, it is also true that the Latino population is widely diverse and marriages with non-Latinos is common. Thus, the full spectrum of the Latino population may include those who do not primarily self-identify as Latino or those who have mixed heritage. Nonetheless, self-identification as Latino is commonly used in research, replacing methods of identification by language and Spanish surname, including for Census enumerators (Ramirez, 2004).

Discussion of Findings

The sexual victimization reported by this sample was substantial with 17.2% reporting any lifetime sexual assault. Sexual victimization was predominantly fondling (11.4%), followed by attempted sexual assault (8.9%), and completed sexual assault (8.8%). These figures show that Latino women who suffered sexual victimization, were often sexually victimized in more than one way—48% of sexual victims reported more than one type of sexual victimization. Sexual assault primarily occurred in childhood (12.2% of the sample reported sexual assault in childhood) by familial or otherwise known assailants. This pattern is common in the general population (Finkelhor, 1990) and is especially pronounced among Latino girls (Arroyo, Simpson, & Aragon, 1997; Clemmons, et al., 2003; Feiring, Coates, & Taska, 2001; Huston, Parra, Prihoda, & Foulds, 1995; Ferol E. Mennen, 1994; Shaw, Lewis, Loeb, Rosado, & Rodriguez, 2001). Adult sexual victimization largely occurred at the hands of a partner/spouse or other known person. Again, this trend is echoed in the general population and has also been found in prior research among Latino women (Van Hightower, Gorton, & DeMoss, 2000). These findings highlight the risk Latino women face in their families and relationships, often at early ages. Both the young victimization and the familial/intimate relationships with the perpetrators likely work to increase psychological harm and decrease help-seeking efforts.

90

The extent of sexual victimization reported in this sample is comparable to other large-scale studies including the National Violence Against Women (NVAW) study. The NVAW and SALAS include sexual assault and attempted sexual assault. The LTVH as employed in SALAS also asks about touching of private parts or sexual fondling, thus including a wider range of unwanted sexual activity than the NVAW. In turn, we also find a higher lifetime sexual victimization rate of 17.2%, than the NVAW (14.6% for Latino women). The rates of sexual victimization found in SALAS are lower than help-seeking samples (Hazen & Soriano, 2007; Roosa, Reinholtz, & Angelini, 1999), geographically limited samples (I. Brown & Schormans, 2003) or college samples (Arroyo, et al., 1997; Clemmons, et al., 2003; Ullman & Filipas, 2005; Urquiza & Goodlin-Jones, 1994) that focus on certain segments of the Latino population. Nonetheless, the issue of sexual victimization represents a significant problem in the Latino population, affecting nearly 2,955,327 women, using our finding as an estimate of the population.

Researchers have established that sexual victimization during childhood is a risk factor for later sexual victimization (Briere & Elliott, 2003; Classen, et al., 2005; Nishith, et al., 2000; Urquiza & Goodlin-Jones, 1994; Wyatt, Guthrie, & Notgrass, 1992), further impacting the lives of child sexual victims. Addressing this research finding directly, SALAS found that child sexual victimization was related to an increased risk of adult sexual victimization. Moreover, experiencing childhood sexual victimization was related to a significantly elevated risk of adult victimization across all victimization types. That is, child sexual abuse was related not only to adult sexual revictimization, but also to physical, stalking, threat and witnessed victimization in adulthood. In fact, the highest odds ratio was not for the link between CSA and adult sexual victimization (4.31) but between child sexual abuse and threatened victimization (4.56). Here, our findings show that mixed type revictimization may be as or more common than same victimization type revictimization. This cross-type revictimization assessment is rarely a focus within the victimization literature.

Risk associated with sexual victimization is further compounded by the fact that the large majority (87.5%) of sexual victims also experience other forms of victimization within the same time period. For SALAS, we designated between childhood and adult sexual victimization. The most common co-occurring victimization during childhood is physical—47.3% of child sexual victims also experienced physical victimization. Among a help-seeking sample the rate of comorbid victimization has been as high as 73% (Mennen, 1994) and 42% of victimized participants in a college sample (author tabulation from Clemmons, DiLillo, Martinez, DeGue, & Jeffcot, 2003). During adulthood, the most common co-occurring form of victimization is threatened violence—55.9% of adult sexual victims also experienced threats. For the victimized women, 61.3% of them experienced more than one type of victimization in their lifetime. Clearly, a narrow focus on sexual victimization misses the complexity of victimization.

Formal help-seeking was not a common response among the majority of sexual victims. In fact, only 1 in 5 sought formal help-seeking avenues defined as medical care, police involvement, social service agency, restraining order, or criminal charges. Other studies have borne out the low levels of formal help-seeking (Dutton, Orloff, & Hass, 2000; West, et al., 1998) often pointing to limited personal resources and cultural isolation. Responses to victimization are shaped by institutional response, personal strengths and resources, tangible resources and social support, personal historical factors, additional life stressors, and positive aspects of the relationship with the abuser (Dutton, 1992). The lack of material resources available to Latino women may hinder help-seeking efforts in that economic ties to intimate perpetrators may limit options. The SALAS sample demographics also point to this: 63% with

high school education or less, about a third of the sample employed full-time, and 68% of

households with incomes below $30,000. Compound this economic and educational

marginalization with linguistic isolation (i.e., 76% preferring the Spanish language for

communication), and the pattern of low formal help-seeking becomes more logical.

The formal help-seeking responses of the participants do show a pragmatic response to

victimization. Medical care was the most often type of help sought among injured sexual

victims, signaling that formal help-seeking is sought when needed for immediate physical harm.

In addition, help-seeking increased as victimization increased underscoring a logical, step up

approach to responding to victimization (Gondolf, Fisher, & McFerron, 1988; West, et al., 1998).

Informal help-seeking was more frequent than formal help-seeking with a majority

(58.3%) of respondents talking to friends or family about their victimization. Yet, looking at the

help-seeking profiles of Latino sexual victims, 35.5% reported no help-seeking, 43.6% reported

informal only, 6.2% reported formal only, and 14.7% reported both. A sizeable portion of these

victims of sexual assault are not talking to anyone about their victimization. Other analyses, not

presented here, show that childhood victimization is especially likely to be associated with no

help-seeking (Sabina, Cuevas, & Schally, under review). This lack of disclosure, which is

consistent with prior research on the underreporting of sexual violence (Arroyo, et al., 1997;

Finkelhor, et al., 1990; Romero, Wyatt, Loeb, Carmona, & Solis, 1999) may further isolate

sexual assault victims.

Cultural factors played a role in both experience of sexual victimization and responses,

pointing to the need of a culturally-embedded analysis. Immigrant status is associated with a

decrease in odds of sexual victimization, such that immigrants are *less likely* to report sexual victimization. In fact, Latinos who adopted an Anglo orientation are at *increased* risk for any sexual victimization and more incidents of sexual victimization. Other studies found similar trends with women born in the US or having higher levels of acculturation, reporting higher levels of CSA (N. L. Brown, et al., 2003; Lira, Koss, & Russo, 1999) sexual victimization (N. L. Brown, et al., 2003), dating violence (Sanderson, Coker, Roberts, Tortolero, & Reininger, 2004) and IPV (Garcia, et al., 2004; Harris, et al., 2005; Jasinski, 1998; Kaufman Kantor, et al., 1994; Lown & Vega, 2001; Mattson & Rodriguez, 1999). A number of factors can explain this relationship. Traditional Latino culture may be protective of victimization due to the importance afforded family and family members. This familism coupled with a clear delineation of appropriate gender roles, may actually decrease the risk of infringement on these patterns. From the Americanization point of view, changing cultural values and roles create stress on the family unit, called acculturative stress, which has been found to increase the risk for victimization (Caetano, Ramisetty-Mikler, Vaeth, & Harris, 2007). Indeed, if the American cultural values stress independence, as opposed to interdependence; antagonism, as opposed to compliance and deference; and selfishness as opposed to sacrifice; the frictions between Latino and Anglo values may ignite violence. While this is a simplistic, generalized assertion, it is true that adaption to a new set of cultural values is a difficult process. Another possibility is that non-immigrant Latinos come to understand themselves within the racial stratification system as minorities, whereas immigrant Latinos may have a sense of themselves as majority members. The stress associated with a minority status and discrimination may increase sexual victimization. For sociologist Ogbu the conditions under which one finds herself as a minority- voluntarily (most immigrants) or involuntarily (US born minorities) influences adjustment and outcomes such as academic performance. Such a dynamic may also influence violence. These assertions are not without support in the literature where other researchers have found a similar connection

between cultural factors and victimization (Garcia, et al., 2004; Harris, et al., 2005; Jasinski,

1998; Kaufman Kantor, et al., 1994) as well as cultural factors and mental health functioning

(Canino & Alegria, 2009; Rogler, Cortes, & Malgady, 1991). An alternative methodological

explanation is also plausible; American born Latino women may be more likely to disclose

victimization in response to a phone survey than foreign-born Latino women given the cultural

emphasis on familial privacy.

Anglo orientation also predicted formal help-seeking even when controlling for number

of victimizations, and immigrant status (see also Cortina, 2004; Lipsky, Caetano, Field, &

Larkin, 2006; Romero, et al., 1999). This may underscore cultural-fit where it is more socially

acceptable to tell unknown persons about personal experiences and to seek social services within

mainstream American culture, but not within traditional Latino culture. Alternatively, Anglo

acculturation may be associated with help-seeking due to having greater knowledge and

opportunity about formal resources and how to gain access to them (e.g., knowing how to get a

restraining order or being proficient in English which expands available social services).

Sexual victimization was significantly predictive of depression, anxiety, anger,

dissociation, and PTSD. This finding supports prior research and underscores the negative long-

lasting effects of victimization. However, when we included total victimization, that is,

victimization beyond sexual, the effect of sexual victimization alone was no longer significant.

This finding echoes earlier trends regarding the importance of evaluating multiple forms of

victimization (Banyard, et al., 2001; Finkelhor, et al., 2007a; Higgins & McCabe, 2001; Maker,

Kemmelmeier, & Peterson, 2001; Nishith, et al., 2000). While sexual victimization predicts

psychosocial functioning when entered alone, introducing other victimizations eliminates the effect. Thus, it is the total amount of victimization here, comprehensively, that is impacting psychosocial functioning. This finding suggests that the effects of sexual victimization may be missing the mark and that models that fail to take into account other victimization experiences possibly overestimate the contribution of sexual violence on psychological distress.

Implications for Policy and Practice

Sexual victimization is common, occurring among 1 in 6 Latino women and is often perpetrated by family members or intimates. For victims of sexual violence, consistent with prior research (e.g., Finkelhor, 1990; Tjaden & Thoennes, 2000) most of the sexual violence experienced in childhood and adulthood is perpetrated by a known assailant with a small percentage of child sexual victimization being at the hands of a stranger. Although also a minority, the rate of sexual violence by strangers is notably higher for victims of sexual assault in adulthood. Services need to be attentive to these dynamics and the difficulties one may face understanding the disconnect between familial/intimate relationships and sexual abuse.

Moreover, what we find is that sexual assault victims are likely to experience either revictimization or polyvictimization, further increasing the negative ramifications of victimization. Clinically, we need to broaden the assessment of Latino women's victimization profile. Victimized individuals will likely seek out treatment as a result of an acute traumatic event and/or experiencing problematic psychological distress with increased victimization increasing the chances that they will seek out formal service outlets. We need to assess the full scope of victimizations that someone may have experienced to adequately develop and use treatment interventions.

These results call into question the organization of services as they developed in the U.S. Sexual abuse services and hotlines are often separated from domestic violence services and hotlines. What is likely true however, is that these two camps are serving the same group of people. The "victim specialization" of services may actually be discouraging to those seeking help if their complex victimization experiences do not seem to cleanly fit domestic violence or sexual assault services. Shifting these services to more broadly reflect the spectrum of victimization experiences may promote women's willingness to take a first step toward formal help-seeking.

Criminal justice interventions were rarely sought among the sample. Only 6.6% called the police, 7.2% sought a restraining order and 6.3% filed criminal charges. Moreover, the follow-up to these responses points to further ineffectiveness. Calling the police resulted in a report and arrest, for slightly less than half of the victims that called the police. Given the commonality of mandatory arrest policies, we might expect a larger number of calls to result in arrest. Indeed the main suggestion of sexual victims who called the police was to arrest the perpetrator (23%). Furthermore, 1 in 3 women who reported getting a restraining order, said their assailant violated the restraining order. While about half of the criminal charges lead to convictions/guilty pleas and sentencing, possibly as a testament to no drop policies, this represents only 3% of all the sexual index victimizations reported. Moreover, rating of satisfaction with criminal justice responses shows room for improvement. Women who used the services reported that they wanted their report to be taken more seriously, get treatment suggestions, and receive legal help. The issue of volition and voice within the criminal justice system needs to be questioned (Goodman & Epstein, 2008). In these regards, culturally competent Spanish-speaking victim advocates may be beneficial, by providing personalized information and walking victims through the legal system. Moreover, outreach is also needed to the Latino community. With fear of offender as a commonly cited reason for not seeking legal remedies, it is important to communicate potential protections to victims.

One of the most opportune points of intervention, according to the responses from SALAS, appears to be medical settings. The Sexual Assault Nurse Examiner (SANE) model, primarily advanced and researched by Rebecca Campbell, provides an excellent intervention point for helping Latino women victims of sexual assault. Her findings show a substantial benefit to using trained nurse examiners with victims of sexual assault in the general population. SANE programs, which deliver patient-focus care and often work cooperatively with rape crisis centers and victim advocates, increase rates of prosecution and police referrals (R. Campbell, 2008). Expanding this resource to work with diverse, potentially monolingually Spanish, populations by increasing bilingual, culturally-competent nurse examiners would mark a beginning to increasing service access to Latino victims of sexual assault. Along these lines, Zarate (2001) suggests an interpreter if SART members are not bilingual and that examiners are sensitive to differences within the Latino community with regard to country of origin, acculturation, and dialect. Furthermore, SART programs should be careful to separate themselves from INS and work with immigrant advocacy groups (Zarate, 2001).

Traditional domestic violence services were uncommonly sought among this population—only 3.3% of sexual victims went to abuse counseling, shelters, domestic violence counseling or called a crisis line. That leaves the large preponderance of victims without these specialized services. One potential reason is the lack of domestic violence/ sexual assault services in Spanish. Indeed, even in Texas, with a relatively high percentage of Latinos, two-thirds of domestic violence organizations reported difficultly serving Spanish-speaking clients (Fitzgerald, 2003). Groups such as the Latina Alliance Against Sexual Aggression, argue for the need of bilingual services, providers who match the demographics of clients, and measurement of bilingual services. Results from the current study echo the need for Spanish services, but knowledge of services in also needed. With a public awareness and educational focus, sexual assault and domestic violence services could counteract the apparent lack of knowledge about the availability of these services. These efforts may be family-based instead of individual-based, as is the current practice. For instance, efforts may educate Latino women how to respond should someone in their family experiences victimization. Indeed, as informal disclosure to family is the most common form of help-seeking, this population may be especially beneficial in informing victims about services (see also Dutton, et al., 2000).

Latino women who did not seek services commonly cited shame, wanting to keep the incident private, and fear. More concerted efforts that address psychological and cultural barriers in addition to language barriers to help-seeking are needed. A focus on preserving the family, stigmatization of divorce, fear and shame oftentimes surface in qualitative studies examining help-seeking behavior (Bauer, Rodriguez, Quiroga, & Flores-Ortiz, 2000; Kelly, 2006; Lewis, et al., 2005; Lira, et al., 1999). These debilitating effects of these reactions is likely exacerbated by cultural components that contribute to this shame as traditional Latino culture places a high value on women's virginity and associates virginity with families' honor. The cultural icon of womanhood as the Virgin Mary may signal to women that sexual behavior is impure, especially non-voluntary sexual behavior. Formal help-seeking venues need to send clear messages that encourage disclosure by recognizing the experience of shame and not letting it translate to self-blame while discouraging the tendency for secretiveness and privacy. That is, cultural sensitivity and responsiveness is needed in service provision, so that these concerns are taken seriously and addressed.

The two main help-seeking profiles include no help-seeking and informal help-seeking only, constituting about 80% of the sample. The ramifications of victimization are diverse and can be long-lasting. Without any linkages to services, these women are left to their psychological strength and social support as the main buffers against mental health and physical health consequences. Further compounding the issue, victimized women may have fewer social resources (Denham, et al., 2007). Domestic violence and sexual assault services, as the main specialized services available to women, need to extend themselves into the Latino community. These post-assault services may become incredibly supportive and recuperative to the victims, but if improperly or insensitively delivered, these services may further victimize women (R. Campbell, 2008).

We should not be quick to accept a view of hesitancy toward help-seeking based on immigration status alone. In fact, immigration status itself did not predict help-seeking responses. The general pattern here focuses on psychological factors in help-seeking, not immigration status itself. This was an unexpected finding given the importance placed on immigration status in the literature, by researchers and service providers alike. The immigration status most likely to influence formal help-seeking is probably undocumented legal status given the fear of deportation. We cannot test this directly, however, since few respondents were categorized as undocumented. Broadly speaking, cultural values, acculturation and psychological impediments such as shame, may play a larger role in help-seeking than immigration status per se. These findings remind us that while there are differences between groups with regards to responses to victimization, victimization itself is consistently linked to internalizing behaviors across groups that need to be addressed. Cultural variables may influence the way ramifications of victimization are played out, but the victimization experience at the hands of family members and intimate partners is a tragic, destabilizing event for all victims, regardless of ethnicity.

Much of the research with Latino women in the past has focused on specific forms of victimization such as physical violence or sexual assault, and how it contributes to psychological distress. However, our results indicate, as others have suggested with non-Latino samples (e.g., Finkelhor, et al., 2007a; Higgins & McCabe, 2000a, 2000b), that this single victimization focus in the research may overestimate the psychological impact of specific forms of victimization. This indicates that the research among Latino women that focused on specific forms of victimization may be inflating the victimization - psychological distress link. This does not suggest that sexual violence does not negatively affect Latino women, but that without evaluating the full spectrum of victimization experiences, it is unclear as to how other victimizations fuel the psychological distress reaction.

Implications for Future Research

The reported figures also suggest that the focus of victimization research directed at Latino women needs to expand beyond its historical emphasis on physical violence and sexual assault. Our data shows that stalking, threat victimization, and witnessed violence are commonly occurring forms of victimization that Latino women experience, at rates equal to, or greater than the rates for physical and sexual assault. Prior research that has emphasized physical violence and sexual assault may be overlooking the larger scope of Latino women's victimization experiences.

The need for a comprehensive assessment of victimization is imperative for valid measurement. Our findings on rate of each victimization, revictimization and polyvictimization all pointed to the significant overlap between victimization. Sexual violence is not the only issue faced by sexual assault victims. Child sexual victims are at equivalent risk for other types of victimization in adulthood besides sexual victimization. In fact, sexual victims are likely to experience multiple co-occurring victimization, what we have termed polyvictimization. Others in the field have begun calling for this comprehensive assessment, showing, as we do, that risk is highest for people who experience these multi-time period and multi-victimization type (Finkelhor, et al., 2007a; Kessler, Molnar, Feurer, & Appelbaum, 2001). Indeed, the concept of complex trauma applies aptly to these patterns.

The importance of measuring and modeling multiple victimizations was apparent in the finding that the effect of sexual victimization on psychosocial functioning was eradicated when total victimization count was introduced. That is sexual assault ceased being a unique predictor of psychosocial functioning. Furthermore, by examining victimization comprehensively, research can more accurately measure women's lived victimization experience, adding more validity to studies. This practice is recommended for future research studies.

Stalking victimization was common among sexual victims as 30% of child sexual victims and 48% of adult sexual victims also reported stalking. While multi-type victimizations are understudied, the studies that do exist generally exclude stalking, focusing instead on physical, sexual, and psychological victimization. Given the high overlap with sexual victimization and the high level of stalking victimization generally found in the sample, further research needs to examine the dynamics of stalking as they relate to Latino women. Are Latino women at higher risk for stalking? How do cultural scripts of man as sexual aggressor play into stalking?

An unfortunate finding needs to be followed-up in future studies. Formal help-seeking was not associated with psychosocial outcomes among sexual abuse victims. Informal help-seeking protected only against depression. Perhaps too many extraneous variables impact recent psychosocial outcomes such as work stress, social support, major life events, etc. Perhaps since counseling was an unlikely help-seeking response, we should not expect a positive association between formal help-seeking and psychosocial outcomes. Conversely, these services may not provide the support and help needed to address personal distress experienced as a result of sexual victimization. Some research shows that at least certain groups of victims who receive substandard care report higher levels of PTSD than those who do not seek services (J. C. Campbell & Soeken, 1999; Filipas & Ullman, 2001). Furthermore, if informal help-seeking efforts are meet with victim-blaming or disbelief, they may negatively impact psychosocial functioning (Filipas & Ullman, 2001).

In order to better understand the low prevalence of criminal justice help-seeking responses, it is important to collect additional detail on the process of this type of help-seeking from availability of interpreters to the level of understanding of the US criminal justice system. Researchers and service-providers both advocate for Spanish-language services for Latino women, yet this continue to be a barrier for Latino women. Future studies could directly examine the difficulties of providing these services and how to better address them.

SALAS offers much insight to the victimization experiences of adult Latino women. Other segments of the Latino population including children, adolescents and adult males also warrant research attention. Beyond capturing prevalence rates, it is important to understand the development and trajectories of violence in Latino's lives, which likely begin at an early age and continue in adult relationships. The experience and impact of dating violence, for example, likely set the stage for future victimization. Latino male adolescents who are victimized themselves by their parents, or witness violence in their homes, neighborhoods, and schools may be learning violent norms that will continue into their relationships. The study of victimization trajectories along with the understanding of the complexity of the victim-perpetrator roles are

important advances for the family violence field that has done well in documenting and

understanding violence with a cross-sectional lens.

V. REFERENCES

Adames, S. B., & Campbell, R. (2005). Immigrant Latinas' conceptualizations of intimate partner violence. *Violence Against Women, 11*, 1341-1364.

American Association for Public Opinion Research. (2009). Standard definitions: Final dispositions of case codes and outcome rates for surveys (6th ed., pp. 50). Deerfield, IL: AAPOR.

American Psychiatric Association. (2000). *Diagnostic and statistical manual of mental disorders* (4th - Text Revision ed.). Washington, D.C.: Author.

Anderson, G., Yasenik, L., & Ross, C. A. (1993). Dissociative experiences and disorders among women who identify themselves as sexual abuse survivors. *Child Abuse & Neglect, 17*, 677-686.

Arata, C. M. (2002). Child sexual abuse and sexual revictimization. *Clinical Psychology: Science and Practice, 9*, 135-164.

Banyard, V. L., Williams, L. M., & Siegel, J. A. (2001). The long-term mental health consequences of child sexual abuse: An exploratory study of the impact of multiple traumas in a sample of women. *Journal of Traumatic Stress, 14*, 697-715.

Barrio, C., Palinkas, L. A., Yamada, A.-M., Fuentes, D., Criado, V., Garcia, P., et al. (2008). Unmet needs for mental health services for Latino older adults: Perspectives from consumers, family members, advocates, and service providers. *Community Mental Health Journal, 44*, 57-74.

Basile, K. C., Arias, I., Desai, S., & Thompson, M. P. (2004). The differential association of intimate partner physical, sexual, psychological, and stalking violence and posttraumatic stress symptoms in a nationally representative sample of women. *Journal of Traumatic Stress, 17*, 413-421.

Bauer, H. M., Rodriguez, M. A., Quiroga, S. S., & Flores-Ortiz, Y. G. (2000). Barriers to health care for abused Latina and Asian immigrant women. *Journal of Health Care for the Poor and Underserved, 11*, 33-44.

Bauman, S. (2005). The reliability and validity of the Brief Acculturation Rating Scale for Mexican Americans-II for Children and Adolescents. *Hispanic Journal of Behavioral Sciences, 27*, 426-441.

Beere, C. A. (1990). *Gender roles: A handbook of tests and measures.* Westport, CT: Greenwood Press, Inc.

Bem, S. L. (1981). *Bem Sex Role Inventory Manual.* Menlo Park, CA: Mind Garden.

Blanchard, E. B., Jones-Alexander, J. B., Buckley, T. C., & Forneris, C. A. (1996). Psychometric properties of the PTSD checklist (PCL). *Behavior Research and Therapy, 34*, 669-673.

Block, C. R. (2000). *Chicago women's health risk study (Part I and II), final report.* (NCJ 183128). Washington, DC: United States Department of Justice.

Blumberg, S. J., & Luke, J. V. (2009). Wireless substitution: Early release of estimates from the National Health Interview Survey, July-December 2008 (pp. 11). Hyattsville, MD: National Center for Health Statistics.

Boney-McCoy, S., & Finkelhor, D. (1995). Prior victimization: A risk factor for child sexual abuse and for PTSD-related symptomatology among sexually abused youth. *Child Abuse & Neglect, 19*, 1401-1421.

Briere, J. (1995). *Trauma Symptom Inventory (TSI) professional manual.* Odessa, FL: Psychological Assessment Resources.

Briere, J. (1996). Psychometric review of the Trauma Symptom Inventory. In B. H. Stamm (Ed.), *Measurement of stress, trauma, and adaptation* (pp. 381-383). Lutherville, MD: Sidran Press.

Briere, J., & Conte, J. (1993). Self-reported amnesia for abuse in adults molested as children. *Journal of Traumatic Stress, 6*, 21-31.

Briere, J., & Elliott, D. M. (2003). Prevalence and psychological sequelae of self-reported childhood physical and sexual abuse in a general population sample of men and women. *Child Abuse & Neglect, 27*, 1205-1222.

Briere, J., Woo, R., McRae, B., Foltz, J., & Sitzman, R. (1997). Lifetime victimization history, demographics, and clinical status in female psychiatric emergency room patients. *Journal of Nervous and Mental Disease, 185*, 95-101.

Briggs, L. (1997). What determines post-traumatic stress disorder symptomatology for survivors of childhood sexual abuse? *Child Abuse & Neglect, 21*(6), 575-581.

Brown, I., & Schormans, A. F. (2003). Maltreatment and life stressors in single mothers who have children with developmental delay. *Journal of Developmental Disabilities, 10*, 61-66.

Brown, N. L., Wilson, S. R., Kao, Y.-M., Luna, V., Kuo, E. S., Rodriguez, C., et al. (2003). Correlates of sexual abuse and subsequent risk taking. *Hispanic Journal of Behavioral Sciences, 25*, 331-351.

Browne, A., & Finkelhor, D. (1986). Impact of child sexual abuse: A review of the research. *Psychological Bulletin, 99*, 66-77.

Buckley, T. C., Blanchard, E. B., & Hickling, E. J. (1996). A prospective examination of delayed onset PTSD secondary to motor vehicle accidents. *Journal of Abnormal Psychology, 105*, 617-625.

Cabassa, L. J. (2003). Measuring acculturation: Where we are and where we need to go. *Hispanic Journal of Behavioral Sciences, 25*, 127-146.

Cabassa, L. J., Zayas, L. H., & Hansen, M. C. (2006). Latino adults' access to mental health care: A review of epidemiological studies. *Administration and Policy in Mental Health and Mental Health Services Research, 33*, 316-330.

Caetano, R., Ramisetty-Mikler, S., Vaeth, P. A. C., & Harris, T. R. (2007). Acculturation stress, drinking, and intimate partner violence among Hispanic couples in the U.S. *Journal of Interpersonal Violence, 22*, 1431-1447.

Callahan, K. (2003). Psychological assessment of adult survivors of childhood sexual abuse within a naturalistic clinical sample. *Journal of Personality Assessment, 80*(2), 173-184.

Campbell, J. C., & Soeken, K. L. (1999). Forced sex and intimate partner violence: Effects on women's risk and women's health. *Violence Against Women, 5*, 1017-1035.

Campbell, R. (2008). The psychological impact of rape victims' experiences with the legal, medical, and mental health systems. *American Psychologist, 63*, 702-717.

Canino, G. J., & Alegria, M. (2009). Understanding psychopathology among adult and child Latino population from the United States and Puerto Rico: An epidemiologic perspective. In F. A. Villarruel, G. Carlo, J. M. Grau, M. Azmitia, N. J. Cabrera & T. J. Chahin (Eds.), *Handbook of U.S. Latino psychology: Developmental and community-based perspectives* (pp. 31-44). Thousand Oaks, CA: Sage Publications, Inc.

Classen, C. C., Palesh, O. G., & Aggarwal, R. (2005). Sexual revictimization: A review of the empirical literature. *Trauma, Violence, & Abuse, 6*, 103-129.

Clemmons, J. C., DiLillo, D., Martinez, I. G., DeGue, S., & Jeffcot, M. (2003). Co-occurring forms of child maltreatment in adult adjustment reported by Latina college students. *Child Abuse & Neglect, 27*, 751-767.

Comas-Diaz, L., & Fontes, L. A. (1995). Puerto Ricans and sexual child abuse. In L. Aronson Fontes (Ed.), *Sexual abuse in nine North American cultures: Treatment and prevention.* (pp. 31-66). Thousand Oaks, CA, US: Sage Publications, Inc.

Cuellar, I., Arnold, B., & Maldonado, R. (1995). Acculturation rating scale for Mexican Americans-II: A Revision of the original ARSMA Acale. *Hispanic Journal of Behavioral Sciences, 17*, 275-304.

Cuevas, C. A., Bollinger, A. B., Vielhauer, M. J., Morgan, E. E., Sohler, N. L., Brief, D. J., et al. (2006). HIV/AIDS cost study: Construct validity and factor structure of the PTSD Checklist in dually diagnosed HIV-seropositive adults. *Journal of Psychological Trauma, 5*(4), 29-51.

Denham, A. C., Frasier, P. Y., Hooten, E. G., Belton, L., Newton, W., Gonzales, P., et al. (2007). Intimate partner violence among Latinas in eastern North Carolina. *Violence Against Women, 13*, 123-140.

Desai, S., Arias, I., Thomson, M. P., & Basile, K. C. (2002). Childhood victimization and subsequent adult revictimization assessed in a nationally representative sample of women and men. *Violence and Victims, 17*, 639-653.

DiNitto, D. M., Busch-Armendariz, N. B., Bender, K., Woo, H., Tackett-Gibson, M., & Dyer, J. (2008). Testing telephone and web surveys for studying men's sexual assault perpetration behaviors. *Journal of Interpersonal Violence, 23*, 1483-1493.

Dutton, M. A. (1992). Assessment and treatment of post-traumatic stress disorder among battered women. In D. W. Foy (Ed.), *Treating PTSD: Cognitive-behavioral strategies. Treatment manuals for practitioners.* (pp. 89-98). New York: Guilford Press.

Dutton, M. A. (1996). Battered women's strategic response to violence: The Role of context. In J. L. Edleson & Z. C. Eisikovits (Eds.), *Future interventions with battered women and their families* (pp. 105-124). Thousand Oaks: Sage Publications.

Dutton, M. A., Orloff, L. E., & Hass, G. A. (2000). Characteristics of help-seeking behaviors, resources and service needs of battered immigrant Latinas: Legal and policy implications. *Georgetown Journal on Poverty Law and Policy, 7*, 1-77.

Elliott, D. M., Mok, D. S., & Briere, J. (2004). Adult sexual assault: Prevalence, symptomatology, and sex differences in the general population. *Journal of Traumatic Stress, 17*, 203-211.

Filipas, H. H., & Ullman, S. E. (2001). Social reactions to sexual assault victims from various support sources. *Violence and Victims, 16*, 673-692.

Finkelhor, D. (1990). Early and long-term effects of child sexual abuse: An update. *Professional Psychology Research and Practice, 21*, 325-330.

Finkelhor, D., Hamby, S. L., Ormrod, R. K., & Turner, H. A. (2005). The Juvenile Victimization Questionnaire: Reliability, validity, and national norms. *Child Abuse & Neglect, 29*, 383-412.

Finkelhor, D., Hotaling, G., Lewis, J. A., & Smith, C. (1990). Sexual abuse in a national survey of adult men and women: Prevalence, characteristics, and risk factors. *Child Abuse & Neglect, 14*, 19-28.

Finkelhor, D., & Ormrod, R. K. (2001). Factors in the underreporting of crimes against juveniles. *Child Maltreatment, 6*, 219-229.

Finkelhor, D., Ormrod, R. K., & Turner, H. A. (2007a). Poly-victimization: A neglected component in child victimization. *Child Abuse & Neglect, 31*, 7-26.

Finkelhor, D., Ormrod, R. K., & Turner, H. A. (2007b). Re-victimization patterns in a national longitudinal sample of children and youth. *Child Abuse & Neglect, 31*, 479-502.

Fitzgerald, A. (2003). *Se habla espanol? Accessibility of services for spanish-speaking clients at domestic violence agencies*. University of Texas at Austin. Austin, TX. Retrieved from www.arte-sana.com/accessibility_spanish_speaking_clients.pdf

Frieze, I. H. (1983). Investigating the causes and consequences of marital rape. *Signs, 8*, 532-553.

Garcia, L., Hurwitz, E. L., & Kraus, J. F. (2004). Acculturation and reported intimate partner violence among Latinas in Los Angeles. *Journal of Interpersonal Violence, 20*, 569-590.

Gelles, R., & Straus, M. (1988). *Intimate violence: The causes and consequences of abuse in the American family*. New York, NY: Simon & Schuster.

Golding, J. M. (1994). Sexual assault history and physical health in randomly selected Los Angeles women. *Health Psychology, 13*(2), 130-138.

Golding, J. M., Stein, J., Siegel, J. M., Burman, M. A., & Sorenson, S. B. (1988). Sexual assault history and use of health and mental health services. *American Journal of Community Psychology, 16*, 625-644.

Gondolf, E. W., Fisher, E., & McFerron, J. R. (1988). Racial differences among shelter residents: A comparison of Anglo, Black, and Hispanic battered women. *Journal of Family Violence, 3*, 39-51.

Goodman, L. A., & Epstein, D. (2008). *Listening to battered women: A survivor approach to advocacy, mental health, and justice.* Washington, DC: American Psychological Association.

Gorcey, M., Santiago, J., & McCall-Perez, F. (1986). Psychological consequences for women sexually abused in childhood. *Social Psychiatry, 21*, 129-133.

Guzman, B. (2001). The Hispanic population: Census 2000 brief. Washington, D.C.: U.S. Census Bureau.

Harris, R. J., Firestone, J. M., & Vega, W. A. (2005). The interaction of country of origin, acculturation, and gender role ideology on wife abuse. *Social Science Quarterly, 86*, 463-483.

Heath, V., Bean, R., & Feinauer, L. (1996). Severity of childhood sexual abuse: Symptom differences between men and women. *The American Journal of Family Therapy, 24*(4), 305-314.

Higgins, D. J., & McCabe, M. P. (2000a). Multi-type maltreatment and the long-term adjustment of adults. *Child Abuse Review, 9*, 6-18.

Higgins, D. J., & McCabe, M. P. (2000b). Relationships between different types of maltreatment during childhood and adjustment in adulthood. *Child Maltreatment, 5*, 261-272.

Hill, P. C., & Pargament, K. I. (2003). Advances in the conceptualization and measurement of religion and spirituality: Implications for physical and mental health research. *American Psychologist, 58*, 64-74.

Idler, E. L., Musick, M. A., Ellison, C., George, L., Krause, N., Pargament, K., et al. (2003). Measuring multiple demensions of religion and spirituality for health research: Conceptual backgroud and findings from the 1998 General Social Survey. *Research on Aging, 25*(4), 327-365.

Ingram, E. M. (2007). A comparison of help seeking between Latino and non-Latino victims of intimate partner violence. *Violence Against Women, 13*, 159-171.

Jasinski, J. L. (1998). The role of acculturation in wife assault. *Hispanic Journal of Behavioral Sciences, 20*, 175-191.

Kaufman Kantor, G., Jasinski, J. L., & Aldarondo, E. (1994). Sociocultural status and incidence of marital violence in Hispanic families. *Violence and Victims, 9*, 207-222.

Kendall-Tackett, K. A., Williams, L. M., & Finkelhor, D. (1993). Impact of sexual abuse on children: A review and synthesis of recent empirical studies. *Psychological Bulletin, 113*, 164-180.

Kessler, R. C., Molnar, B. E., Feurer, I. D., & Appelbaum, M. (2001). Patterns and mental health predictors of domestic violence in the United States: Results from the National Comorbidity Survey. *International Journal of Law and Psychiatry, 24*, 487-508.

Kessler, R. C., Sonnega, A., Bromet, E., & Hughes, M. (1995). Posttraumatic stress disorder in the National Comorbidity Survey. *Archives of General Psychiatry, 52*, 1048-1060.

Lewis, M. J., West, B., Bautista, L., Greenberg, A. M., & Done-Perez, I. (2005). Perceptions of service providers and community members on intimate partner violence within a Latino community. *Health Education & Behavior, 32*, 69-83.

Liang, B., Goodman, L., Tummala-Narra, P., & Weintraub, S. (2005). A theoretical framework for understanding help-seeking processes among survivors of intimate partner violence. *American Journal of Community Psychology, 36*(1/2), 71-84.

Lipsky, S., & Caetano, R. (2007). The role of race/ethnicity in the relationship between emergency department use and intimate partner violence: Findings from the 2002 National Survey on Drug Use and Health. *American Journal of Public Health, 97,* 2246-2252.

Lira, L. R., Koss, M. P., & Russo, N. F. (1999). Mexican American Women's Definitions of Rape and Sexual Abuse. *Hispanic Journal of Behavioral Sciences, 21,* 236-265.

Lown, E. A., & Vega, W. A. (2001). Prevalence and predictors of physical partner abuse among Mexican American women. *American Journal of Public Health, 91,* 441-445.

Mattson, S., & Rodriguez, E. (1999). Battering in pregnant Latinas. *Issues in Mental Health Nursing, 20,* 405-422.

McFarlane, J., Wiist, W., & Watson, M. (1998). Characteristics of sexual abuse against pregnant Hispanic women by their male intimates. *Journal of Women's Health, 7,* 739-745.

Mennen, F. E. (1994). Sexual abuse in Latina girls: Their functioning and a comparison with White and African American girls. *Hispanic Journal of Behavioral Sciences, 16,* 475-486.

Mennen, F. E. (1995). The relationship of race/ethnicity to symptoms in childhood sexual abuse. *Child Abuse & Neglect, 19,* 115-124.

Merrill, L. L., Guimond, J. M., Thomsen, C. J., & Milner, J. S. (2003). Child sexual abuse and number of sexual partners in young women: The role of abuse severity, coping style, and sexual functioning. *Journal of Consulting and Clinical Psychology, 71,* 987-996.

Neumann, D. A., Houskamp, B. M., Pollock, V. E., & Briere, J. (1996). The long-term sequelae of childhood sexual abuse in women: A meta-analytic review. *Child Maltreatment, 1*, 6-16.

Nishith, P., Mechanic, M. B., & Resick, P. A. (2000). Prior interpersonal trauma: The contribution to current PTSD symptoms in female rape victims. *Journal of Abnormal Psychology, 109*, 20-25.

Pargament, K. I., Koenig, H. G., & Perez, L. M. (2000). The many methods of religious coping: Development and initial validation of the RCOPE. *Journal of Clinical Psychology, 56*, 519-543.

Perilla, J. L., Bakerman, R., & Norris, F. H. (1994). Culture and domestic violence: The ecology of abused Latinas. *Violence and Victims, 9*, 325-339.

Pew Research Center. (2005). Hispanics: A people in motion. Washington, D.C.: Pew Research Center.

Phinney, J. S., & Flores, J. (2002). "Unpackaging" acculturation: Aspects of acculturation as predictors of traditional sex roles attitudes. *Journal of Cross-Cultural Psychology, 33*(3), 320-331.

Raj, A., & Silverman, J. (2002). Violence against immigrant women: The roles of culture, context, and legal immigrant status on intimate partner violence. *Violence Against Women, 8*, 367-398.

Ramirez, R. R. (2004). We the people: Hispanics in the United States *Census 2000 Special Reports*. Washington, D.C.: U.S. Census Bureau.

Rogler, L. H., Cortes, D. E., & Malgady, R. G. (1991). Acculturation and mental health status among Hispanics: Convergence and new directions for research. *American Psychologist, 46*, 585-597.

Romano, E., & De Luca, R. V. (2001). Male sexual abuse: a review of effects, abuse characteristics, and links with later psychological functioning. *Aggression and Violent Behavior, 6*, 55-78.

Sabina, C., Cuevas, C. A., & Schally, J. L. (under review). Help-seeking in a national sample of victimized Latino women: The influence of victimization type.

Salmon, C. T., & Nichols, J. S. (1983). The next-birthday method of respondent selection. *Public Opinion Quarterly, 47*, 270-276.

Sanders-Phillips, K., Moisan, P. A., Wadlington, S., Morgan, S., & English, K. (1995). Ethnic differences in psychological functioning among black and latino sexually abused girls. *Child Abuse & Neglect, 19*, 691-706.

Sanderson, M., Coker, A. L., Roberts, R. E., Tortolero, S. R., & Reininger, B. M. (2004). Acculturation, ethnic identity, and dating violence among Latino ninth grade students *Preventive Medicine: An International Journal Devoted to Practice and Theory, 39*, 373-383.

Sedlak, A. J., & Broadhurst, D. D. (1996). *Third national incidence study of child abuse and neglect*. Washington D.C.: Department of Health and Human Services.

Sorenson, S. B., & Telles, C. A. (1991). Self-reports of spousal violence in a Mexican-American and non-Hispanic White population. *Violence and Victims, 6*, 3-16.

Spertus, I. L., Yehuda, R., Wong, C. M., Halligan, S., & Seremetis, S. V. (2003). Childhood

emotional abuse and neglect as predictors of psychological and physical symptoms in

women presenting to a primary care practice. *Child Abuse & Neglect, 27*, 1247-1258.

Tjaden, P., & Thoennes, N. (2000). Full report of the prevalence, incidence, and consequences of

violence against women. Washington, D.C.: U. S. Department of Justice, Office of

Justice Programs.

Torres, S., & Campbell, J. C. (1998). Intervening with battered Hispanic pregnant women

Empowering survivors of abuse: Health care for battered women and their children. (pp.

259-270). Thousand Oaks, CA, US: Sage Publications, Inc.

Trickett, P. K. (1998). Multiple maltreatment and the development of self and emotion

regulation. *Journal of Aggression, Maltreatment, and Trauma, 2*, 171-187.

Tyler, K. (2002). Social and emotional outcomes of childhood sexual abuse. A review of recent

research. *Agression and Violent Behavior, 7*(6), 567-589.

U.S. Census Bureau. (2000). American FactFinder. Retrieved 8/9/2009

U.S. Department of Health and Human Services. (2001). Mental health: Culture, race, and

ethnicity - A supplement to mental health: A report of the Surgeon General. Rockville,

MD: U.S. Department of Health and Human Services,.

U.S. Department of Health and Human Services. (2008). Child maltreatment 2006. Washington

DC: U.S. Government Printing Office.

Urquiza, A. J., & Goodlin-Jones, B. L. (1994). Child sexual abuse and adult revictimization with

women of color. *Violence and Victims, 9*, 223-232.

Valentine, S., & Mosley, G. (2000). Acculturation and sex-role attitudes among Mexican

 Americans: A longitudinal analysis. *Hispanic Journal of Behavioral Sciences, 22*, 104-

 113.

Van Hightower, N. R., Gorton, J., & DeMoss, C. L. (2000). Predictive models of domestic

 violence and fear of intimate partners among migrant and seasonal farm worker women.

 Journal of Family Violence, 15, 137-154.

Vasquez, M. J. T. (1998). Latinos and violence: Mental health implications and strategies for

 clinicians. *Cultural Diversity and Mental Health, 4*, 319-334.

Weathers, F. W., Litz, B. T., Herman, D. S., Huska, J. A., & Keane, T. M. (1993). *The PTSD*

 Checklist (PCL): Reliability, validity, and diagnostic utility. Paper presented at the

 International Society for Traumatic Stress Studies, San Antonio, TX.

West, C. M., Kaufman Kantor, G., & Jasinski, J. L. (1998). Sociodemographic predictors and

 cultural barriers to help-seeking behavior by Latina and Anglo American battered

 women. *Violence and Victims, 13*, 361-375.

Widom, C. S., Dutton, M. A., Czaja, S. J., & DuMont, K. A. (2005). Development and validation

 of a new instrument to assess lifetime trauma and victimization history. *Journal of*

 Traumatic Stress, 18, 519-531.

Widom, C. S., & Morris, S. (1997). Accuracy of adult recollections of childhood victimization:

 Part 2. Childhood sexual abuse. *Psychological Assessment, 9*, 34-46.

Wolfe, D. A. (1994). Factors associated with the development of posttraumatic stress disorder

 among child victims of sexual abuse. *Child Abuse & Neglect, 18*(1), 37-50.

Wyatt, G. E., Guthrie, D., & Notgrass, C. M. (1992). Differential effects of women's child sexual abuse and subsequent revictimization. *Journal of Consulting and Clinical Psychology, 60*, 167-173.

Zarate, L. (2001). Suggestions for upgrading the cultural competency skills of sexual assault response teams Retrieved January 15, 2010, from http://www.arte-sana.com/articles/suggestions_upgrading_article.htm

www.ingramcontent.com/pod-product-compliance
Lightning Source LLC
Chambersburg PA
CBHW081327310526
45789CB00018B/2448